The Visual History of
Costume Accessories

Original research and text for the
Costume Accessories series used in
the compilation of this volume:

Hélène Alexander   *(Fans)*
Fiona Clark   *(Hats)*
Valerie Cumming   *(Gloves)*
Jeremy Farrell   *(Umbrellas & Parasols; Socks & Stockings)*
Vanda Foster   *(Bags and Purses)*
Alice Mackrell   *(Shawls, Stoles and Scarves)*
Diana Scarisbrick   *(Jewellery)*

THE VISUAL HISTORY OF
COSTUME ACCESSORIES

Valerie Cumming

BT Batsford Ltd London

Printed in Hong Kong for the publishers

BT Batsford Ltd
583 Fulham Road
London SW6 5BY

www.batsford.com

A catalogue record for this book is available from
the British Library.

0 7134 7375 4

Contents

Acknowledgements

The idea for this book was suggested in the early 1990s and I am grateful to various colleagues at Batsford, past and present, especially Richard Reynolds and Martina Stansbie, for persevering with it. Their encouragement has always been most welcome.

I am, as always, indebted to many individuals and organizations for their assistance in providing advice and suggestions on both content and illustrations. My former colleagues at the Museum of London have been particularly helpful, most notably in regard to new illustrations. That Museum's collection provides a superb resource for all books on costume and accessories.

My especial thanks go to those authors of the original Costume Accessories series who allowed me to use some of their work; I recommend all readers of this book who have a specialist interest in one or more type of accessory to return to those small but valuable volumes.

As always, I am deeply appreciative of my husband's support for a distracted author.

Preface

The idea behind the Costume Accessories series was to provide short, well-illustrated primers for students, collectors and curators who need basic information about specific types of accessory. In certain instances they complement recent publications on the subject; others are the only reliable guide to the subject matter. All of them are widely available in public, college and museum libraries; most of the titles in the series can still be obtained from specialist second-hand book dealers.

The success of the compendium volume, *The Visual History of Costume* (based on six volumes), suggested that an overview is helpful, and that a similar formula might be applied to accessories. Also, and this meets a criticism levelled at the visual histories, the content illustrates many surviving examples rather than emphasizing the appearance of dress as recorded by artists, sculptors, caricaturists and the like. The major disadvantage in this approach is that the condition of the surviving examples and their visual presentation is extraordinarily varied. Some accessories have an innate ability to look both appealing and informative, for example, fans and jewellery. Others, such as gloves, shawls, stockings and shoes, rarely seem convincing when divorced from the contours of the human body. However, as this is the state in which curators, collectors and students see them for much of the time, this aesthetic quirk will be understood by the majority of readers who use this book.

Once the book started to take shape, it became apparent that a rather different emphasis and format were needed to give coherence to diverse items which either evolved slowly or show such subtle changes that it is easier for readers interested in meticulous detail to consult the original books. Also, for many reasons, it was necessary to use a number of very different examples - these, I hope, add a freshness to this volume. There are a number of interesting connections to be made by considering motifs, patterns, influences across the range of accessories, and I hope these provide another dimension for the reader to consider. The balance of the book tends to emphasize female accessories because of their range and variety. Also, because the twentieth century is so well documented in other books on dress and accessories, and the rate of change is so fast, the book ends just after the middle of the century. The last fifty years are represented by a few iconic images, but in truth need a volume of their own, exploring the rise of informality, the international acceptance of sportswear as a source for ideas on dress and accessories, and the boom in luxury, designer-labelled goods.

This book is not about the history of dress *per se*, for that the reader can go to *The Visual History of Costume* or more detailed studies on a particular period. Beyond the introduction the format is akin to the visual histories with each illustration having a detailed caption which draws upon both caption and textual information from the original volumes. Certain elements have been omitted: descriptive information which is easy to see in the illustration, sizes, and technical language unless this is absolutely essential to comprehension. A detailed glossary doubles as an index, and there is a list of collections to visit, and a bibliography.

It is important to reiterate the point that this is one author's individual view of accessories, and it considers their role as conveyors of stylistic innovation or ingenuity rather than as examples of technical change. I am particularly grateful to those authors who let me use some of their material, but any solecism in this book is mine.

List of illustrations

1. **Richard Sackville, 3rd Earl of Dorset (1589-1624)**
   William Larkin, 1613
   Ranger's House, Blackheath, London;
   English Heritage

2. **Men's nightcaps, c. 1600-1620**
   Museum of Costume and Textiles, Nottingham

3. **Gaming purses, French, c. 1590-1620**
   Museum of London

4. **Hawking furniture, c. 1603-1619**
   Burrell Collection, Glasgow

5. **Lady Dorothy Cary**
   William Larkin, c. 1614
   Ranger's House, Blackheath, London;
   English Heritage

6. **Girl's shoe, c. 1600**
   Ashmolean Museum, Oxford

7. **Youth's shoe, c. 1605-1613**
   Aylesbury Museum

8. **Henry Rich, 1st Earl of Holland (1590-1649)**
   studio of Daniel Mytens, 1632-33
   National Portrait Gallery

9. **Glove, 1630-40**
   The Museum of Costume, Bath; collection, the
   Worshipful Company of Glovers

10. **Galerie du Palais**
    Abraham Bosse, c. 1637
    BT Batsford Ltd Archive

11. **Man's hat, c. 1650**
    Courtesy of the trustees of the Victoria and
    Albert Museum, London

12. **Stockings, English, c. 1650**
    Manchester City Art Galleries

13. **Man's boothose, English, c. 1650-1680**
    Courtesy of the trustees of the Victoria and
    Albert Museum, London

14. **Lady Walking in the Countryside**
    engraving by Jean de St Jean after Nicholas
    Bonnart, 1676
    Pepys Library, Magdalen College Cambridge

15. **Drawstring purses, English, c. 1660-1680**
    Museum of London

16. **Woman's mule, c. 1660-1665**
    Museum of London

17. **Le Magasin des Modes**
    engraving by Jean Berain, 1678
    Witt Library, Courtauld Institute of Art

18. **Men's gloves, 1660-1680**
    The Museum of Costume, Bath; collection, the
    Worshipful Company of Glovers

19. **Men's mules, 1670-1680**
    Museum of London

20. **Men's gloves, 1680-1700**
    The Museum of Costume, Bath; collection, the
    Worshipful Company of Glovers

21. **Letter case or pocket book, 1687**
    Museum of Leathercraft, Northampton

22. **Man's shoe, 1680-1690**
    Museum of London

23. **Queen Mary II (1662-1694)**
    engraving, 1692-1694
    BT Batsford Ltd Archive

96. **Woman's bonnet, English, 1840-50**
City Museum and Art Galleries, Stoke-on-Trent

97. **Parure, English, c. 1850**
Museum of London

98. **Woman's shawl, English, 1840-60**
Worthing Museum and Art Gallery

99. **Women's mittens and a fan, 1840-45**
Manchester City Art Galleries

100. **Two parasols, English, 1844-50**
Museum of London

101. **Fan, ?French, 1851**
Museum of London

102. **Men's socks, English, 1830-40**
Museum of Costume and Textiles, Nottingham

103. **The Empty Purse**
James Collinson, 1857
Tate Gallery

104. **Cartoon from Punch, 1855**
Worthing Library

105. **Parasol, English, 1855-65**
Manchester City Art Galleries

106. **Shawl, English, c. 1850**
Norfolk Museums Service

107. **Reticule, English, c. 1850**
Manchester City Art Galleries

108. **Stocking, English, 1851**
Museum of Costume and Textiles, Nottingham

109. **Women's boots, c. 1850**
Museum of London

110. **To Brighton and Back for 3/6**
Charles Rossiter, 1859
Birmingham Museum and Art Gallery

111. **Advertisement from a paper bag, c. 1860**
BT Batsford Ltd Archive

112. **Cartoon from Punch, 1866**
Worthing Library

113. **Shawl, Scottish, c. 1865**
Courtesy of the trustees of the Victoria &
Albert Museum

114. **Gig umbrella, 1860-1900**
Museum of Costume and Textiles, Nottingham

115. **Engraving from Girl of the Period, July 1869**
Museum of Costume and Textiles, Nottingham

116. **Pair of 'pork pie' hats, 1860-65**
Manchester City Art Galleries

117. **Hats, English, 1868-70**
Manchester City Art Galleries

118. **Square parasol, c. 1869**
Derby City Museum and Art Galleries

119. **Women's gloves and purse, 1860-70**
Manchester City Art Galleries

120. **Women's stockings, c. 1865 and 1879**
Museum of London

121. **Women's shoes, 1860-1870**
Museum of London

122. **From the Milliner, Dressmaker and
Warehouseman's Gazette, July 1874**
Museum of Costume and Textiles, Nottingham

List of colour plates

Introduction

There are three basic concepts which inform consideration about human appearance: form, function and fashion. The human body or form needs, for reasons of survival, to acquire coverings of one kind or another. These can be functional: to protect and warm the body and to shield it from the harmful effects of excessive sunshine or extremes of cold; to prevent important extremities such as hands and feet from being damaged by the natural environment through contact with sharp stones, thorns, predatory insects and animals and natural poisons. The short step from function to fashion is quickly made by the inventive human mind, especially if non-functional and transitory fashions can be devised or purchased which express status and also enhance the outer appearance for the pleasure of the wearer and his or her circle. There will be other factors which influence both function and fashion: economic, religious and moral to name the most obvious. In the period covered by this book all play a significant part although moral and religious strictures tend to be considered under the catch-all heading of etiquette.

For the purposes of identifying significant changes to accessories they are considered in relationship to high fashion or, when appropriate, as a traditional style which attained an almost uniform status, for example, the man's top hat in the nineteenth century. It should not be forgotten, however, that nearly all of the accessories discussed in this book had their early origins in function rather than fashion. Head coverings, gloves, stockings and shoes fulfilled a protective role. Fans, parasols and umbrellas allowed individuals to attempt to mitigate adverse climatic conditions, albeit in a primitive manner. Bags were derived from the simple leather pouches within which small valuable items and money could be carried close to the body. Jewellery developed from the simple pins and brooches which held garments together. Shawls, scarves, cravats and ties might be considered on the margins of functionality but it can be argued that both assist in retaining body heat for women and men respectively. In passing, it should be noted that not every category of accessory is included in the published series but in this volume, when appropriate, they are mentioned.

There is a shifting hierarchy of importance amongst accessories. Certain items undergo periods of stasis, others change constantly and not all need regular renewal or improvement. The selection of images is intended to reflect these shifts in significance and, in the following paragraphs a synoptic view will be given, century by century. The conclusion which will be drawn is that footwear is the overall winner on grounds of function. It is true today and could have been true in the past that although all other accessories are attractive they are non-essential extras. Without footwear, most human activity in the western world would have been curtailed or impossible to undertake. But on grounds of fashion, that is another story...

Seventeenth-century accessories

The selection of accessories which survive from the seventeenth century is intended to illustrate the tension between decoration and simplicity which characterized the appearance of both men and women. Later, it will become apparent that male accessories stabilize, achieving an almost uniform conservatism. However, in this awkward century in which aspects of post-medievalism and an embryonic modernism jostle together for pre-eminence, the accessories of both sexes are of equal interest and, sometimes, are impossible to identify as specifically male or female.

Decoration found expression in the widespread use of intricate pattern, embroidery, applied ribbons and lace; all, except the last, exuberantly colourful. In part this was a necessity – the lack of technical innovation meant that cutting and fit were relatively crude and surface embellishment disguised this fact rather well. In addition, the surface decoration could suggest wealth, the ability to acquire and wear fabrics and designs chosen from a growing range of goods imported from Europe and the Near and Far East.

All of the accessories which are discussed in this book were available in Europe and North America at some point in the century although a few were mere curiosities, such as parasols and umbrellas. In England the first third of the century produced a range of highly embroidered articles: caps and coifs, sashes, gloves, purses and sweetbags, and stockings. These drew their inspiration from published herbals and bestiaries which were full of unusual (and sometimes inaccurate) depictions of flora and fauna, known, exotic and imaginary. Coloured silks, gold and silver thread, seed-pearls and spangles were used to recreate, in miniature, a quasi-natural world of heartsease (pansies), carnations, roses, leaves, insects, birds and mammals with a droll disregard for respective sizes. The slow speed of technical advance in manufacturing throughout the century allowed a mixture of professional and amateur production to co-exist. There were exceptions: the making of hats, jewellery, gloves, fans and shoes required tools and craft skills which were beyond the reach of all but a few especially talented amateurs, and lace-making took some time to become an amateur occupation. The fine Italian reticella lace with its complex geometric patterns and, later in the century, the sinuous, delicate designs of Flemish and French lace were in demand because of their comparative rarity and difficulty of emulation.

By the second third of the century it was becoming increasingly apparent that the French hegemony in matters to do with fashion was spreading far beyond the borders of France. Although there was resistance to this in England and elsewhere (in Holland, for example), through informal insularity or state prohibition on certain types of import, the growing strength of France as a political, economic and mercantile power, was felt throughout Europe and beyond. England, France and Holland became the key players in the international arena with jealously guarded new trading links with North America, India and the East and West Indies. Both England and Holland had developed idiosyncratic styles of dress in the late sixteenth and early seventeenth centuries, but whereas the former was increasingly influenced by the French style of dress, less flamboyant, and more restrained and elegant in appearance, the Dutch took only those elements of luxurious accessory which suited their manner of life. Also, through their trading links, the Dutch ensured the growing popularity of Indian and Chinese designs and goods, quickly adjusting the specifications to meet European tastes in materials, embroideries and china. The English, always eclectic in their tastes, happily absorbed oriental influences: 'tree of life' designs for embroidery, gauzy Indian scarves with metallic threads, and printed Indian cottons became more popular as the century progressed.

The sense of restraint imposed upon English society by the triumph of the parliamentarians, the execution of Charles I in 1649 and the establishment of a Commonwealth in 1652 was marked but short-lived. Conspicuous show was reduced, but the desire for choice in matters to do with personal appearance found renewed expression after the restoration of the monarchy in 1660. An exuberant frivolity can be seen in the profusion of uses to which ribbons, lace, fringe and surface decoration was put in the last third of the century. However, and this was a significant change, there was a gradual but perceptible drawing apart between the range, style and design of accessories for men and women.

Looking at the possibilities from top to toe, a simple, almost formulaic style of hat developed for men which, from the 1680s, was no longer worn indoors. Instead wigs became a dominant feature of masculine appearance and remained so for almost 150 years; caps were worn only in informal circumstances. In contrast, women's caps became complex confections of gauze and lace and, out of doors were topped by a hat or protected by a parasol; only young, unmarried girls could escape such head-coverings. Men's jewellery reduced to an almost minimal level compared with earlier in the century; a watch, ring, shoe buckles, and, on formal occasions, a chain or order of chivalry and jewelled detachable buttons. Women wore earrings, jewelled pins, brooches, bracelets, rings; these were usually plain pearls and gold and certainly not in such profusion except on formal occasions when suites of diamonds or other gemstones, set in gold, twinkled from the ears, neck, bosom and fingers. Men's lace cravats and sleeve ruffles became less flamboyant as women's increased in scale, often with the addition of scarves, tippets and light shawls of silk, gauze, lace or fur. Both sexes wore gloves but again they differed in style and use; men's were practical, for riding or other outdoor activities and highly decorated only on formal occasions. Women's gloves were lighter, longer and prettily embroidered or decorated with silk tufts and worn for long periods of time both in and out of doors. Neither sex had yet developed a taste for the known (through depiction and description) European curiosities of parasol and umbrella but women admired and used, with growing frequency, fans of English and European origin.

Drawstring purses and lettercases were used by men and, to a lesser extent, by women; the latter much preferred tie-pockets worn under their skirts or work bags which held needlework necessities. Both sexes wore stockings which, from the 1670s, had gore clocks to ensure a better fit when knitted on a frame, but it is difficult to distinguish from colour or decoration whether there were different tastes for men and women. This is not the case with footwear. Sturdy boots and plain leather shoes with latchets characterized male footwear whilst women who could afford it eschewed plain leather for embroidered silk, velvet or brocade shoes with high heels.

Acquiring such finery was an expensive if enjoyable business. The principal English city for luxury goods throughout the century was London. Here could be found the range of goods and skilled craftsmen to which no other city could aspire. Goldsmiths, silkmen, lacemen, glovers, fanmakers were carefully regulated by strong guilds (called Livery Companies) and were located in various streets or areas of the square mile of the City of London and, as the boundaries of London extended west and east, in Soho, Covent Garden and Spitalfields. As well as supplying customers in London they provided a service to smaller provincial tradesmen and to pedlars and journeymen who travelled to country fairs with the latest novelties. There was a thriving second-hand clothes business and, to judge from advertisements in the *London Gazette*, a strong black market in stolen goods of every type and description. Goods could be made to order but there was much that could be bought ready-made. As London was a port there was the possibility of ordering from overseas and ensuring that unusual or exotic goods were on show before they reached other parts of the country. Knowledge of the newest styles and changes in taste was assisted, from the 1670s onwards, by the publication in Paris of the latest fashions worn at the French court.

Introduction

Eighteenth-century accessories

Although there is no obvious reason for dividing the discussion of accessories into centuries, such a division does help an understanding of currents of continuity and patterns of change. The simplicity of masculine appearance which had evolved in the late seventeenth century continued, with certain notable exceptions which are outside the range of this survey. At court or at grand receptions men wore fine lace, enamelled watches, diamonds and embroidered stockings but, more generally, and to the surprise of many foreign visitors, Englishmen were so plainly dressed as to be almost indistinguishable from their servants. Strong, bright colours found their way into men's dress on formal occasions but the simplicity of their accessories was the rule rather than the exception. Plain black beaver three-cornered hats with discreet metal lace trimming, simple linen cravats, light tan gloves, white silk stockings and plain black leather shoes with small metal buckles are depicted in quantity in contemporary paintings, and the limited survivals of such accessories tend to reinforce the visual evidence. Even when men started to use umbrellas in the 1780s these were made of sombre, dark green material. Only the changing styles of wig suggest wit and ingenuity. However, accessories often survive because they are unusual, highly wrought or valuable. Such survivals provide evidence of a fascination for exquisitely decorated watches, delicately beaded purses, and sets of breeches and shoe buckles in every type of metal and stone: precious and semi-precious. Gentlemen usually wore swords and, on occasion, carried a cane but these accessories, like wigs, are beyond the remit of this book except to be commented on when they are depicted in contemporary illustrations.

If, relatively speaking, it was a quiet century for men's fashions, it was the reverse for women's. Caps became exquisite towers of lace and gauze called commodes, modestly subsided into discreet ovals with lappets, were replaced by pompons of flowers and jewels and then overtaken by quasi-oriental turbans and blowsy mob-caps perched on distortedly high and wide structures of real and artificial hair surmounted by wide-brimmed hats. The traditional jewellery of pearls for earrings and necklaces was augmented by sets of precious stones which included flamboyant rows of stomacher clasps for formal occasions. Good-quality paste often fooled those who assumed that what they saw were family heirlooms. Lace was worn in caps, around the neck, across the shoulders, as sleeve ruffles, and trimming delicate aprons. Fur tippets added warmth in winter and gloves and mittens were made in seasonal fabrics: silk for summer and leather for winter decorated with embroidery or inset panels of lace. Fans became part of the vocabulary of etiquette, their movements and position – open, half-open, shut – all conveying information. Work bags of silk, for knotting or embroidery were widely used and carried. Stockings diminished from brightness to simpler pastel shades with embroidered clocks as the century ended, and were increasingly available in fine-quality cotton as well as silk. Shoes were colourful, lightweight and high-heeled until the 1780s when a change occurred to complement the narrower and more simple lines of dresses. Leather and low heels suggested freedom of movement. Alongside umbrellas, women adopted the use of the staff parasol, finally succumbing to this French fashion.

When considered in its entirety the century cannot be perceived, stylistically, as other than a series of movements, some evolutionary, others perversely idiosyncratic. The early eighteenth century retained some of the late Baroque taste of the late seventeenth century. Elaborate decoration acquired a somewhat exotic asymmetry which is most notably found around 1700-1715 in the so-called 'bizarre' silks, but also was an influence in women's caps and men's wigs. As this changed the first indications of Rococo decoration found expression in dress and accessories. Delicate trailing ribbons and more naturalistic floral designs, based upon accurate representations of European specimens and those newly observed from much further away, and a contrived sense of informality, were the essence of French, and to a lesser extent, English dress from the mid-1720s until the early 1760s. For the English this informality was real, it mirrored their enjoyment of eschewing the artificiality of urban life for the much simpler pleasures of country living.

During the last thirty years or so of the eighteenth century there was increased interest in travel and the results of travel. The scholarly could explore the antiquities of Greece and Rome, read about the results of scientific expeditions (such as Captain Cook's, although the science often acted as a fig-leaf for the less palatable economic reasons for such exploration), and take pride in the increasing British influence in India and the West Indies. The loss of the American colonies was mitigated, to a degree, by strong and continuing links of an economic and social nature. The combination of ever-widening trading links and the growing possibilities for travel produced ideas for ornament, design and many products new to western European tastes. One obvious example is the fascination with depictions of antiquity: Roman ruins were painted onto fan leaves and became popular souvenirs of the Grand Tour, as did cameos with subjects from antiquity which soon left the realm of dilettante collectors and were set into jewellery as a natural complement to simpler styles of female dress in the 1790s. Although initially unpopular in France, shawls from Kashmir with the stylized buta design (now incorrectly referred to as Paisley pattern after the nineteenth-century factories whose fortunes were built upon

inexpensive versions using this design) quickly found favour in England in the 1780s. As with all good designs, lively native entrepreneurs quickly produced cheaper variants. James Tassie's catalogue of 1791 promoted his glass reproductions of intaglios and cameos whilst P.J. Knights, a Norwich weaver, was awarded the silver medal of the Society of Arts in 1792 for his counterpane which imitated East India shawl counterpanes. By 1793 he was presenting the 'Norwich Shawl Manufactory Exhibition' in Bond Street and numbered royalty amongst his customers.

This disarming European ability to marry antiquarian styles of jewellery with eastern designs for shawls was very successful, demonstrating yet again the ingenuity of craftsmen and manufacturers when assessing the potential of novelties from every known source of supply. The French Revolution in 1789 and the subsequent periods of terror, disruption and war in France and beyond spread the quasi-democratic ideas quickly. The physical manifestation of the Revolution, or so it seemed, was exhibited in a fascination for the antique world and its supposed simplicity in dress and ornament. Alongside this ran a delight in extremes of colour and pattern. This heady mixture was observed with concern and scepticism by those outside France and either ignored or much toned-down.

Nineteenth-century accessories

Throughout the nineteenth century the development and growth of towns ran in step with technical changes. The range of skills and opportunities needed to equip a growing population with goods of every sort naturally produced a wider choice in the luxury goods market. Seasonal fairs, pedlars and commissions to city cousins or family members visiting such centres diminished as towns expanded and more shops opened to satisfy local or regional demands. The increased productive capacity of inventions in spinning and weaving ensured that more people could acquire basic items of dress cheaply and more regularly. There was a price to be paid for this change and it was in the poor working conditions and social unrest of the population at large. This did not stop the widening of the entrepreneurial middle class and the constant growth in its levels of consumption. The demand for luxurious novelties seemed limitless; this can be measured not just through economic statistics but also through the plethora of specialist magazines, advertisements in newspapers and the introduction of the shopping wonder of mid-Victorian England, the department store, with its catalogues, order forms and delivery service for those unable to visit in person. Alongside this widening social basis for consumption ran a nervous concern about how to dress and how to behave, and there was a consequent demand for books on etiquette. Slender books became encyclopaedic tomes as it became apparent that the newly rich needed advice on every aspect of the life their wealth could buy but which could easily be scorned as arriviste by the old, established gentry and aristocracy. Increased literacy also led to an explosion of sources of information available for purchase in the form of books, magazines and journals but also through subscription libraries. The taste for informative works on science, philosophy and history was challenged by the taste for novels. In a line from Jane Austen, through the 'silver fork' writers such as Bulwer-Lytton and Disraeli to Trollope, George Eliot and beyond, there was a genre which both celebrated and satirized the foibles of fashionable society and those who aspired to be part of it.

In the nineteenth century there was a growing divide between men's clothing and women's. The former became simpler, more businesslike; good tailoring became the key to masculine attire, and the two- or three-piece suit, in its many formal and informal variants, was increasingly worn. There were idiosyncratic young men – 'dandies' in the early years of the century, 'swells' later – who promoted a more imaginative and colourful style of menswear, but they were a tiny minority. Men's accessories were much simpler in line with this relative sobriety, and innovation was slow and discreet. All items from hats to boots took time to change, and the acceptance of umbrellas, top hats, socks rather than stockings, and ties in place of cravats, was incremental rather than immediate. Technical advances ensured that cut, fit and size were more accurate than in preceding centuries. In contrast women's clothes and accessories were constantly changing, and novelty was highly sought after. It was a century in which all of the accessories depicted in this book, and many more not included, were colourful and ingenious in construction and design. Certain items, such as hats, shawls, bags and parasols, became especially significant.

The early years of the century had offered a less constricting style of dress but, by the 1820s, there was a return to the exaggeration of one element of dress or anatomy. Wide shoulders and sleeves, crinolines, bustles and tightly laced corsets emphasized narrow waists for much of the century. There was a layered, overly decorative effect which was enhanced by the addition of accessories to garments already riotous in colour and pattern. Simplicity was not much admired and although seasonal fashion plates might suggest a restrained elegance, in portraits (and from the 1840s onwards, photographs) there is evidence that many women preferred fussiness, adding jewellery, shawls, mittens and fans, none of which seemed co-ordinated. The three most celebrated fashion icons of the second half of the century, the Empress Eugénie of France, the

Empress Elizabeth of Austria and the Princess of Wales, were dressed by the finest *couturiers* but were often overwhelmed by the plethora of accessories available to them.

Certain designs acquired an almost classic status, for example, the so-called Paisley motif, taken from the Indian shawls and popularized by the Scottish manufacturers of such shawls. Certain fabrics, lace being an obvious example, added delicate but fussy prettiness to shawls, parasols and fans, and lacy motifs are found on stockings. Flowers were a popular source of inspiration for decoration on fabrics, on hats, gloves, fans, footwear and for jewellery. Sometimes the floral motifs were delicate, sometimes almost overblown. The widespread introduction of aniline (chemical) dyes in the 1860s allowed a much wider range of colours to be used: bright greens, dazzling pinks, lustrous purples and acidic yellows. At its worst, women's dress had much in common with a cluttered Victorian drawing room, full of colour, texture and unmatched patterns all overlaid by flounces, ruches and beads, an expression of ornament for its own sake. Artistic and dress reform movements tried to introduce simpler, more natural designs, but this was at variance with the prevailing taste which, in those great international exhibitions held from 1851 onwards, rewarded complex ingenuity in everything from furniture to footwear and eschewed classic understatement.

Twentieth-century accessories

The speed of change in all aspects of twentieth-century life is taken for granted, as is the broader base within society to which all sorts of goods and services can be sold. Clothing becomes less cumbersome, and women's dress overtakes that of men in using lighter fabrics, less restrictive styles to allow for greater activity in domestic and working life. Two world wars, the development of new forms of media in which to convey information and the need for women to work were all elements which ensured that stiff etiquette and tightly monitored social roles were eroded. There was still a delight in novelty and a frivolity in dress and accessories, and there were new fabrics and materials with which to experiment. Although the easier, more comfortable styles of clothing often needed fewer accessories, the actual matching and co-ordinating of colour and decoration was more evident; the idea of 'accessorising', that is, putting together shoes, gloves, bag to complement a particular outfit, was promoted through journals and magazines, and seen in the cinema. Inspiration was taken from many sources: art, archaeological discovery, folk dress; humour, and wit and imagination were as much a part of the story as in previous centuries, but fewer accessories were actually required, a situation exacerbated by shortages during wartime.

Mademoiselle Chanel, Rue Cambon, 1966
Photograph: Hatami. Copyright: Chanel

Chanel's enormous contribution to accessories is discussed on pp.158-9.

Femme du jour, en caraco a la Pierrot avec une juppe de taffeta bariolé, recouvert d'un tablier moucheté derriere la juppe
1. 2. 3. Chapeaux a la mode du plus nouveau goût.
A Paris chez Esnauts et Rapilly, rue St. Jacques a la Ville de Coutances. Nᵒ 259. Avec Privilege du Roi.

This French fashion plate of the 1780s captures much of the glamour, ingenuity and wit of fashionable accessories, as well as their ephemeral nature.

THE VISUAL HISTORY OF COSTUME ACCESSORIES

Seventeenth-century accessories

1. Richard Sackville, 3rd Earl of Dorset, William Larkin, 1613

Note: Richard Sackville (1589-1624) was a fashionable and notoriously extravagant courtier in a period during which both men and women at the court of James I (1603-1625) were criticized as dressing in a manner 'more sumptuous than the Persians'.

Hat: An example of the fashionable copotain with a tall, slightly tapered crown and moderate width of brim. This style reached England in the mid-sixteenth century. Copotains were made from a variety of materials. The most popular colour was black, as in this instance. Jewelled brooches or pins and decorative hat bands were usual. The hat was worn tilted to the side or the back.

Gloves: The wardrobe accounts for the clothing worn in this portrait still survive; the cloth of silver gauntlets to his gloves are embroidered in black to match his doublet and shoes. The embroidered gauntlet and leather hand were made separately, then sewn together, the join disguised by the ruched silk ribbon around the wrist.

Stockings: Two pairs of stockings were listed with this outfit: white silk embroidered in gold, silver and black (worn here) and black silk embroidered in gold and silver. The pair of gold and silver lace-edged black taffeta garters were both decorative and practical: they ensured a wrinkle-free lower leg.

Shoes: These match the doublet and gloves and show the higher heel which became fashionable in the late 1590s for both men and women. The extravagant shoe roses disguise the narrow front tongue to which the latchets were fastened.

2. Men's nightcaps, c. 1600-1620

Linen with embroidery in coloured silks and gold thread.

Note: Men wore caps for informal indoor use from the sixteenth to the end of the nineteenth century. Often worn with a loose gown, they were referred to as nightcaps but were not actually worn in bed. In the sixteenth and seventeenth centuries they had a deep round crown made from four conical sections stitched together with the border turned up to make a close-fitting brim.

The form of women's indoor caps derived from the coif (a close-fitting linen bonnet worn by men from the twelfth century onwards). In the early seventeenth century they were usually fastened with a drawstring at the neck, curving over the cheeks to reveal some side hair but concealing the ears.

Such caps and coifs were often the result of domestic needlework and drew upon patterns published in the herbals and specialized books of designs, or were drawn by itinerant journeymen who visited households in order to provide professional assistance with fashionable embroidery designs. See colour plate I.

3. Gaming purses, French, c. 1590-1620

White kid covered with silk velvet and embroidered with metal thread; plaited metal drawstrings and tassels. The owner's coat of arms was often embroidered on the base to ensure correct identification of the winnings. The stiffened circular base sat flat on the table and the pleated sides held the coins or gaming counters securely. Examples vary in size and although thought to be French in origin (a favourite motif in the embroidery is the fleur-de-lis), they were used in various countries in Europe.

Note: The full skirts and breeches of the late sixteenth and early seventeenth centuries meant that both sexes could conceal a simple leather drawstring pouch beneath their garments. There are, therefore, few illustrations of the types of purse, pouch or sweet-bag which survive in museum collections.

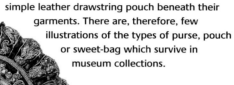

4. Hawking furniture, c. 1603-1619

Tan suede leather with polychrome embroidery in silks and metal thread.

Note: Hawking gloves were made of thick leather, sometimes of double thickness, to ensure that the bird's claws did not pierce the flesh. This style of glove is simpler than that worn by Richard Sackville. The gauntlet is made from one section of embroidered fabric with a flared side gusset, allowing it to fit over the sleeve and cuff without creasing them. The pattern of coiling stems, flowers and fruits is typical of this period. However, the game bag has a metal frame and flared shape more like earlier medieval girdle pouches than the soft, drawstring leather pouches in use by this date.

This hawking furniture is associated with James I whose favourite pursuits were various forms of hunting.

5. Lady Dorothy Cary, William Larkin, c. 1614

Note: The exuberant decoration found on menswear was equalled by that of female contemporaries. The widespread use of lace and embroidery, and certain similarities between their collars, cuffs and footwear are a reminder that the majority of the specialist merchants and craftsmen supplied both sexes at this date, using identical stock for both, the obvious difference being the construction of the principal garments. The metal embroidery on Lady Dorothy's gown should be compared with that on the gaming purses (Fig. 3) and the silk embroidery on her bodice and skirt can be compared with the hawking furniture (Fig. 4).

Cap: Head-coverings ranged from simple coifs to fashionable caps of fine gauze and lace, wired to stand away from the fuller hairstyles of this period. This style combined both modesty and coquettishness and was described by the Venetian Ambassador in 1618 as 'worked bands with fine lace which falling over the forehead form what our Venetian dames term the "mushroom"'.

Jewellery: Pendant gemstones and pearl earrings were fashionable for much of the seventeenth century, and, in the 1620s and 1630s, were worn by men (usually singly) as well as women.

Neckwear: Reticella lace over linen collar, supported on a pickadil. Although less exuberant than that worn by Richard Sackville (Fig. 1), the shape and construction are similar.

Stockings: Turquoise-green silk; the colour is echoed in the centre of the shoe rose. The extravagant use of embroidery on the gown, bodice and skirt suggest that the stockings might have embroidered clocks.

Shoes: White leather with open sides which reveal the stocking. The shoe rose is made from two widths of gold ribbon, a turquoise-green centre and is smothered in spangles.

6. Girl's shoe, c. 1600

White suede punched with chevron bands of decoration between slits incised in the surface of the leather. The open sides would reveal much of the stocking (see Fig. 5). Latchets tie over and through a top pair of holes on the tongue; a second, lower pair of lace holes allowed a shoe rose to be attached.

Note: The perforated chevron decoration mirrors that found on clothing at this date; the portrait of Sir Walter Raleigh and his son, c. 1600 in the National Portrait Gallery, London depicts similar decoration on Sir Walter's trunkhose.

7. Youth's shoe, c. 1605-1613

Brown leather with a wedge heel. The shoe is made 'straight', that is, to fit either foot. It is fastened by latchets tied through a pair of lace holes on the high tongue. A simple incised decoration is found on the surface of the leather.

Note: Shoes began to be made as 'straights' when heels were introduced, although some shoes were made with right and left feet into the 1620s. Lace ties ranged from simple ribbons to the elaborate roses worn by the most fashionable in society.

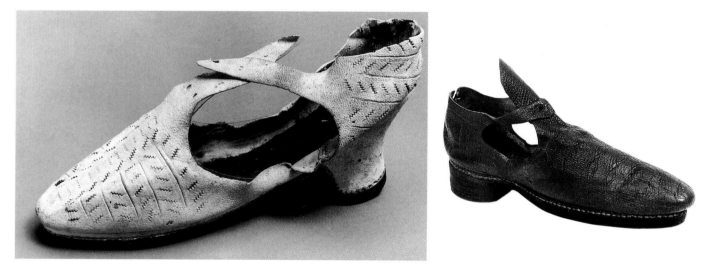

8. Henry Rich, 1st Earl of Holland, 1632-33
studio of Daniel Mytens

Note: Henry Rich (1590-1649) was one of Charles I's courtiers and this full-length portrait epitomizes the restrained grandeur which was associated with the royal court. Like the earlier portrait of Richard Sackville, this contains much useful information about changes to those accessories of which there are few surviving examples.

Hat: In the mid-1620s a new style of hat with a lower crown and wider brim became fashionable. It was made from a soft felt which allowed its brim to be 'cocked' – turned up to right, left, or at the front like a halo – or 'coggled' which formed a wavy line. The trailing plume was a fashionable feature of this style.

Gloves: As the lines and fabrics of men's clothing became more sculptural in the period after 1625, so gloves were simplified to harmonize. Henry Rich's

braided gauntlet gloves with their narrow, bushy fringe are typical of this overall co-ordination of items of dress.

Boothose: These were stockings made to be worn with boots. They were usually plainer at the ankle than ordinary stockings but had flared and decorated tops. The turned-down tops of Rich's linen boothose are trimmed with densely patterned lace in scallops which complement the boot tops.

Boots: The pale suede boots with contrasting brown leather tops and soft, wrinkled legs are typical of 1620-30, although style of top and height of heel varied. The removable protective flat-soled golosh prevented the heel sinking into soft or muddy ground. The butterfly-shaped spur leather protected the ankle from the stirrup.

Henry Rich Earl of Holland .

9. Glove, 1630-40

Mid-brown suede leather decorated with applied bands of pale-blue satin ribbon overlaid with gold and silver gilt thread and trimmed with silver gilt lace and spangles and a silver gilt fringe.

Note: Many of the simpler gauntlet gloves from the late 1620s up to the 1640s survive in museum collections. They were often made in one piece, that is, without the join between hand and gauntlet. The decoration is discreet, with a simple band of embroidery around the outer edge of the gauntlet, narrow outline motifs, or relatively plain bands of decoration, as in this example. Fringed tops were a usual feature of these styles.

10. Galerie du Palais, Abraham Bosse, 1637

Note: This French engraving illustrates both the choice and the manner in which accessories could be acquired. French fashions were influential throughout Europe in the seventeenth century but especially in England where the queen consort, Henrietta Maria, was French.

Hats: The men all wear low-crowned, wide-brimmed felt hats trimmed with feathers; the flexibility of this style, with brims cocked, turned back, or 'coggled', is evident.

Jewellery: Several of the women wear the ubiquitous row of pearls around the neck and two have circular gemstone brooches at the front of their collars. The display behind the counter shows several decorative chains, probably of enamelled precious metal and/or pearls and small gemstones; these were worn by both men and women on formal occasions.

Gloves: The pair of gloves displayed behind the counter are much shorter than was usual in England at this date. They appear to be decorated with a band of ruched ribbon just above the wrist. Both the man and woman in the right foreground are wearing pairs similar to those displayed.

Fans: The woman in the right foreground has a fixed feather fan suspended from her waist, but the folding fans, both on display and being considered by a customer, are more typical of surviving examples of the

mid-seventeenth century. Fans had appeared in Europe a century earlier and those with vellum or paper leaves and carved ivory sticks slotted into the leaf were highly decorated. Subjects for the painted decoration were taken from biblical stories or classical mythology.

Boothose: The three men in the foreground all wear scalloped-edge boothose, probably of linen trimmed with lace.

Boots: The men wear boots with supple leather tops of a width to be pulled down and then taken up to produce a bucket effect just below the knee.

11. Man's hat, c. 1650

Black felt with a tall 'sugarloaf' crown and stiff brim. This style resuscitated the earlier copotain (see Fig. 1) and is popularly associated with Puritans, especially in North America. However, Puritan dress, although less decorative than that of fashionable contemporaries, was not wholly divorced from stylistic changes in silhouette.

Note: A similar style of hat was worn by both sexes. In London it was worn by merchants and street traders long after it ceased to be fashionable. Examples of this hat, worn by the king and his entourage, can be seen in the painting 'Charles II entering the City of London', Dirck Stoop, 1661 (Museum of London).

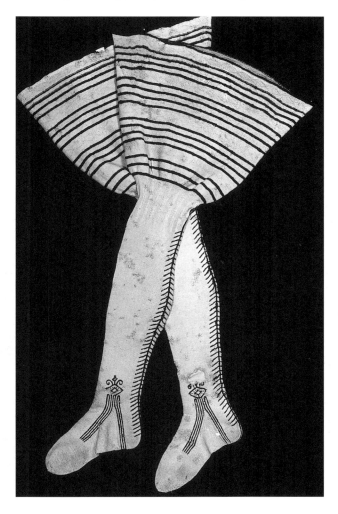

12. Stockings, English, c. 1650

Hand-knitted green silk stocking; silver thread is used to form the chevrons below the welt, the zigzags either side of the centre back, the outline of the clock and the palmette.

Note: Although both men and women wore stockings, there are few illustrations of the differences between the sexes in the choice of stocking. Colours were popular and included red, green and blue in addition to black and white. Stockings were made from silk, linen and worsted thread, and were either knitted, usually by hand until the middle of the century, or cut and sewn from cloth. It is likely that two pairs of stockings were often worn (upper and under hose) for warmth, greater density of colour and opaqueness. In 1647 James Masters paid 19s. for a pair of green silk stockings.

13. Man's boothose, English, c. 1650-1680

Hand-knitted in cream wool with embroidered decoration in navy-blue wool. The hose are knitted in the round with all the decoration on the outside of the cuff; the band of ribbing at the knee would help keep up the cuff and prevent the garter from slipping. How this fine example was held up is uncertain. There is no visible means of support in the way of eyelet holes, and the top decoration would be hidden if they were supported only by the boot cuff; possibly they were pinned to the breeches.

Note: As boot tops could be bought separately, the survival of this fine complete pair of boothose is unusual. The use of wool was, of course, more economical than silk, although half-silk stockings, that is, with wool or linen bottoms, could be worn with separate boot tops. James Masters bought half-silk stockings for 9s. 6d. in 1646. As shoes replaced boots for fashionable wear, particularly after 1660, boothose tended to go out of fashion.

Dame se promenant a la Campaigne

Ce vend à Paris proche les Grands Augustins aux deux Globes a la seconde Chambre Avec Privil du Roy.

J.D. de S.Iean delin.

14. Lady Walking in the Countryside, engraving by Jean de St Jean after Nicholas Bonnart, 1676

Note: Although a number of costume books were published in the sixteenth century and engravings by artists such as Wenceslaus Hollar depicted the changing fashions, it was the French who introduced a regular supply of 'fashion plates' from the late 1660s onwards. They are an important source of information about fashionable dress and accessories.

Hat: A soft hood is tied loosely around the face to which is attached a fine dark veil. Hoods, often made of fine silk, continued to be worn by many women in the late seventeenth century.

Jewellery: A plain row of pearls is the only visible item of jewellery, although the flamboyant ribbon bow attached to a narrow band around one wrist, in the manner of a bracelet, is typical of the use of ribbons found on men's and women's clothing in the 1660s and 1670s.

Gloves: From the late 1630s onwards women had worn longer plainer gloves than men; these covered the arm as sleeves shortened and by the 1670s were usually at least elbow length. The plainest varieties had vertical lines of pointing on the back of the hand, often with decorative silk tufts along the line of the knuckle, as in this example.

Parasol: The parasol, with its turned wood or ivory handle and fringed silk cover, is a noticeable feature of this fashion plate; its appearance suggests that either the stretchers are very short or the parasol is rigid. Although parasols and umbrellas were not unknown, only a few reached England as novelty items. See colour plate III.

Shoes: These have the pointed toes which became fashionable in the late 1660s and are decorated to complement the striped mantua. At much the same time open-sided shoes declined in popularity and women's fabric shoes became closed in structure.

15. Drawstring purses, English, c. 1660-1680

Frog purse (top left) of cream silk overlaid with a mesh of silver thread; the strings control its mouth which acts as a receptacle for coins. The nut purse (top right) is made from two halves of a walnut covered in silk and linked by silk gussets; the embroidery is in silk, silver thread, seed pearls and coral beads. The flat purse (bottom) is of light-blue and silver silk decorated with applied silver lace and edged with salmon-pink ribbons which also form the tassels.

Note: Luxurious novelties were increasingly in evidence towards the end of the seventeenth century; although the complex embroidery skills of the earlier part of the century were used less often, the combination of ingenuity, wit and a lavish use of ribbons and tassels is found on a number of accessories in this period (see Fig. 17).

16. Woman's mule, c. 1660-1665

Crimson velvet embroidered with a scroll and flower design in silver thread and edged with silver braid. The complex embroidery design is typical of the formal, baroque decorative motifs also found on furniture and wall coverings of this date.

Note: This mule slipper is traditionally associated with Queen Henrietta Maria (1609-1669), the widow of Charles I and mother of Charles II (1660-1685).

17. Men's gloves, 1660-1680

At the bottom is a cinnamon coloured doeskin glove with looped decoration consisting of ribbons of green, blue, cream and silver tinsel around the cuff and down the length of the hand; similar to those in Fig. 18. The glove (centre) is made from soft white leather, possibly doeskin, with green stitching outlining the fingers and thumb. A punched decoration of holes and a serrated edge mark the join with the shallow gauntlet which has two bands of dark-green silk ribbon woven through the serrated vertical bands of leather, and two bands of paler-green silk ruched ribbon applied beneath the laced rows. Three ribbon rosettes are applied to the back of the hand, one centred above the fingers and the two smaller ones on the little finger. At top left the glove is of white leather with an applied decoration of silver, white and orange ribbons, the wrist edged with silver gilt lace.

Note: Men's gloves from about the time of the Restoration in 1660 until about 1680 reflected the fashionable interest in surface decoration, principally characterized by an excessive use of looped ribbons, on clothing and accessories alike.

18. Le Magasin des Modes, engraving, Jean Berain, 1678

Note: This engraving appeared in the *Mercure Galant,* a journal noted for its advice to readers on how to dress and where to buy fashionable goods. This interior may be of a shop in the Palais Royal and can be compared to one of c. 1637 (Fig. 10).

Hats: The young woman is wearing a lace cap fitted closely around the head and under the chin with matching lappets. Her escort has a low-crowned, shallow-brimmed hat curled up at one side, an early sign of what was to develop into a cocked hat in the 1690s.

Sashes and scarves: Ornate sashes became a feature of fashionable male dress in the 1670s; they enlivened the otherwise undistinguished, narrow, and somewhat ill-fitting line of the early style of coat. Good examples are displayed amongst the merchandise. The young woman does not seem to be wearing a scarf similar to those displayed at centre left but something more like a tippet. This fur scarf or cravat was reintroduced to the French court by Princess Liselotte von der Pfalz in 1671 when she married Louis XIV's brother Philippe d'Orléans. Initially ridiculed, this novelty was the height of fashion by the mid-1670s.

Gloves: The man is wearing gloves similar to those displayed behind him. These are narrow suede or leather gauntlet gloves with ruched ribbon or fringe decoration. This length fitted neatly under the wide coat cuffs and added a further decorative feature below the braid of the cuffs. The woman has plain elbow-length gloves fitted closely to her arms.

Stockings: The man is wearing a plain pair of stockings, probably in silk to complement the rest of his exquisite appearance. Behind him can be seen ornate petticoat breeches, one pair of which has upper sections of stocking attached, perhaps to be worn with a plainer stocking beneath and the style of boot seen to the right.

Shoes: The style of shoes worn by fashionable women can be seen to the left of the engraving. The high heels, closed sides, high tongues and pointed toes are typical of the late 1670s. The young man's shoes have the long square-toed fronts, high tongues and heels fashionable throughout Europe. Buckles were worn to fasten shoes from the 1660s but were interchangeable with ribbon ties for some years. To the right are depicted Louis XIV's riding boots decorated with rows of gold buttons and an attached and frilled boot top. Soft suede boots in this style were worn more in Europe than in England.

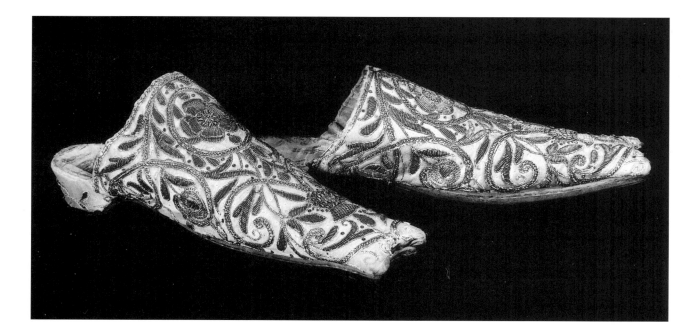

19. Men's mules, 1670-1680

Pink satin embroidered with metal thread and spangles. The high fronts, inverted toes and wedge heels are typical of this period.

Note: Informal dress for men included decorated nightcaps, soft, loose robes, and mules, which were worn in the house as both day and nightwear.

20. Men's gloves, 1680-1700

Buff-coloured suede leather embroidered with silver gilt thread in a stylized floral design with heavy silver gilt fringing interspersed with massive, intricately coiled bullion tassels.

Note: Fringed gloves are depicted in contemporary fashion plates but the thickness and weight of these (two pairs survive in the Spence Collection, Museum of Costume, Bath) suggest that they were for riding and/or ceremonial use. A less ornate pair, in a private collection, was owned by a gentleman of the bedchamber to William III (1688-1702). In the Verney papers a bill for similar gloves gives their cost as £6 7s.

21. Letter case or pocket book, 1687

Brown morocco (goatskin) leather embroidered in silver
wire with a design of scrolling flowers and, under the
front flap 'Saml. Pepys Esq' and on the back
'Constantinople 1687'. This may have been a gift as
Pepys made no recorded visit to the Turkish city in that
year. However, such decorative cases were obviously a
known speciality of Constantinople; the Costume
Museum, Nottingham has a similar example dated 1717
and the Museum of fine Arts, Boston has a richly
embroidered silk one marked 'Constantinople 1755'.

Note: This letter case is associated with the diarist and public
servant Samuel Pepys (1633-1703). Such cases were used to
safeguard letters, papers and bank bills and a fair number survive
in museum collections. Usually envelope-shaped, they were made
in a variety of materials.

22. Man's shoe, 1680-1690

Black leather buckle shoes with narrow straps which
buckled over a high tongue to which a plain or decorative
buckle could be attached to fasten the shoe.

Note: The introduction of decorative shoe buckles: small oblongs or
ovals of metal set with gemstones or paste were, from the outset,
treated as jewellery, to be used with different pairs of shoes.

Maria D.G. Angliæ Scotiæ Franciæ et Hiberniæ Regina. &c

Vandervaart Pinxit.   I. Smith fecit.   Cum Privilegio Regis   Sold by E. Cooper at ye 3 Pidgeons in Bedford Street.

23. Queen Mary II (1662-1694), engraving, 1692-1694

Note: Mary was the daughter of James II but her marriage to her cousin Prince William of Orange-Nassau (later William III) meant that she spent her early adulthood at the Dutch court in the Hague. She had a keen interest in accessories; an account book from 1694 listed expenditure on lace, ribbons, painted fans, sable muffs, gloves and jewellery of diamonds, emeralds and pearls.

Cap: This type of cap became fashionable in the late 1680s when the sides of earlier, smaller caps lengthened into streamers or lappets and the front was formed into several tiers arranged as upstanding pleats or flutes which required the support of a silk-covered frame called a commode. This French fashion displayed to advantage the fine laces and silk ribbons which resulted from the investment by Louis XIV's finance minister Colbert in the production of luxury goods in France.

Jewellery: Drop-shaped pearl earrings and one row of large pearls around the neck were favourites with women of all ages. Large stomacher brooches were worn at the centre of a low-cut neckline. They could be simple in design using the brilliance and quality of finely cut stones to create a dazzling effect, or they used naturalistic floral and leaf designs, enamelwork and a variety of gemstones. Queen Mary owned 'a great jewel of diamonds to be worn before with a large heart diamond in the middle thereof'.

Gloves: Delicate lines of pointing and silk tufts are the only decoration on these elbow-length suede gloves.

Fan: The guard, the outer stick, was usually decorated. This flower and leaf motif is typical of the period.

24. Woman's hat, 1680-1700

Fine cane plaited in openwork patterns with the lower crown and firm, wide brim found in use in the later seventeenth century for men's hats. The intricate pattern echoes the designs found on Italian reticella lace, and this example may be an import from the well-established Tuscan straw-hat industry.

Note: This hat, from the Foley estate, Hereford, is associated with Queen Anne (1702-1714); it is similar in size and manufacture to one associated with Queen Elizabeth I (1558-1603) which is preserved at Hatfield House. The earliest records of the English straw-plaiting industry for hat making date from the late 1670s and by 1688 a petition from straw plaiters in Bedfordshire, Buckinghamshire and Hertfordshire stated that 14,000 people in those counties lived by making straw hats. Depictions of the style of these English hats and surviving examples have yet to be found.

25. Necklace and earrings, 1650-1710

Coques de perles (the central whorl of nautilus shells) backed with mother of pearl in gilt metal collets. Seventeen shells, graduated in size towards the centre, form the necklace from which is suspended a bow set with faceted green paste and seed pearls above a pendant pearl. The earrings are *en suite*.

Note: Pearl jewellery had a long period of popularity and it is often difficult to date closely such classic styles if they lack a firm provenance.

26. Women's gloves, 1685-1710

Three styles of suede and leather embroidered gloves, ranging from the relatively plain, similar to those worn in Fig. 23, to the highly decorated examples. There are similarities between the motifs found on the work bag (Fig. 27) and the glove which is embroidered the entire length of the arm.

27. Work bag, 1699

Linen and cotton twill embroidered in multi-coloured worsteds with a 'Tree of Life', oriental birds and figures, and the date. The reverse has a similar design with the initials 'E.M.'. The bag is edged with fringe and fastened with tasselled drawstrings.

Note: Fine needlework was an accomplishment expected of every well-bred woman and therefore work boxes and work bags were important accessories. Surviving examples seem mostly to have been home-made, giving a date, initials and often using the same sinuous 'Tree of Life' patterns found on many contemporary crewel-work hangings. Such bags were probably used to store the large hanks of blue, green and carmine worsteds used in these embroideries.

PARAPLUYES
ET PARASOLS
A PORTER DANS LA POCHE.

LES Parapluyes dont Mr Marius a trouvé le secret, ne pesent que 5 à 6 onces : ils ne tiennent pas plus de place qu'une petite Ecritoire , & n'embaraffent point la poche; ainfi chacun peut fans s'incommoder en avoir un fur foy par précaution contre le mauvais temps. Ils font cependant auffi grands, plus folides, refiftent mieux aux grands vents, & fe tendent auffi vite que ceux qui fonten ufage.

C'eft le témoignage que Mesfieurs de l'Académie Royale des Sciences en ont rendu.

Cette nouvelle Invention a paru avoir été bien reçue du Public par le grand debit qui s'en eft fait, ce qui a excité l'Auteur à la perfectionner, au point qu'il ne laiffe plus rien à fouhaiter du côté de la folidité.

A l'égard de ceux qui font ornez, l'on conviendra qu'il ne s'eft encore rien vû en Paraffols de plus agréable pour le goût & la légereté, & que l'on peut contenter en ce genre les Curieux les plus difficiles, pour la richeffe des montures & des ornemens. *Ils auront tous fa marque.*

Ils fe font & fe vendent à Paris chez Mr MARIUS, demeurant ruë des Foffez Saint Germain , aux trois Entonnoirs.

Par l'autorité d'un Privilege du Roy, portant deffenfe par toute l'étenduë du Royaume de les contrefaire , à peine de mille livres d'amende.

Il ne faut pas confondre cet Invention avec celle des Parapluyes dont les branches fe mettent dans une Sarbacanne. Ces fortes de Parapluyes ont déplû par leur petiteffe & leur peu de folidité; d'ailleurs il falloit trop de temps pour les tendre.

De l'Imp. de J. C.

Permis d'imprimer & d'afficher
Fait à Paris ce 15. Juin 1715
M. R. de V. D'ARGENSON.

---

28. Advertisement, French, 1715

Note: Depictions and descriptions of umbrellas appeared in England in the late seventeenth century. Oil cloth had been invented in Italy and by 1637 Louis XIII of France owned three umbrellas, as well as eleven parasols. However, early umbrellas do not seem to have survived, although ingenuity in construction obviously exercized early makers as this advertisement indicates.

Umbrella and parasol: The ornate parasol held by the woman and the man's plain umbrella are obviously reduced in size to fit the small bags depicted next to them. This may have been achieved by using a hollow stick, perhaps telescopic or by sections screwing together and whalebone ribs which were probably hinged.

29. Earrings,
possibly European, early eighteenth century

Oval and pear-shaped crystal pendants backed with red and silver foil and set in stylized silver leaves and buds inlaid with tiny crystals.

30. Gloves, 1700-1715

Cream kid embroidered with silver passing thread, woven fringe of torsade silver thread, part lined in blue silk taffeta. These gloves mark the transitional stage between the longer gauntlet gloves of the 1680s and 1690s and the plainer and shorter gloves with a curved open vent at the side which were worn in town early in the eighteenth century.

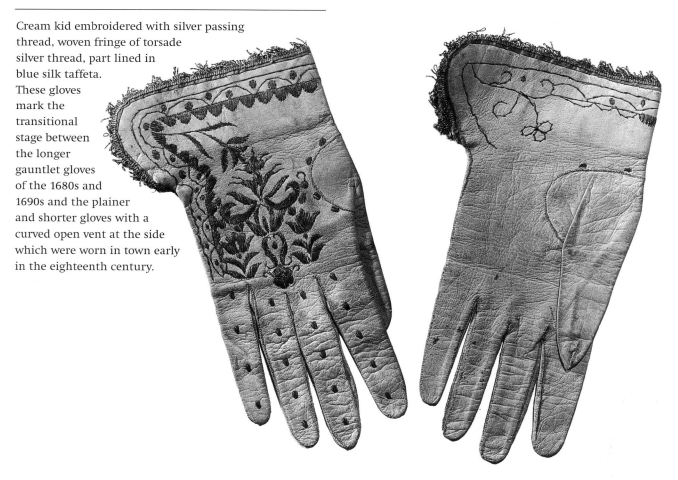

31. Women's mules, 1720-1730

Green silk embroidered with silver thread.

Note: This elegant but somewhat impractical style was a French fashion for indoor wear, though not only on informal occasions.

32. Stockings, 1725-1750

The stocking (left) is of machine-knitted pink silk with a green silk gore clock with plated decoration on each side and at the top. The right-hand stocking is machine-knitted green silk with a pink silk gore clock and plated decoration. The plated decoration was achieved by laying the top colour over the foundation colour.

Note: There seems to have been little difference between the stockings worn by both sexes from the late seventeenth century into the eighteenth century. Gore clocks appeared in the 1670s as a refinement which could enable a better fit for stockings produced on a frame. Wedge-shaped gores, embellished by embroidery and often in contrasting colours are one of the most decorative features in the history of stocking production. Such stockings survive in museum collections in Derby, Manchester and London. Embroidered clocks over self-coloured or contrasting gores were also produced. Silk stockings were expensive, as much as 14s. in 1681 and £1 2s. in 1738/9.

Eighteenth-century accesscries

33. 'The Rake at the Rose Tavern', Scene III of *The Rake's Progress*, 1733, William Hogarth (detail)

Note: Hogarth's works are a particularly fine source of evidence for the details of eighteenth-century life in the period between the early 1720s and 1760. The range of characters he depicted and their appearance in formal, informal and disreputable circumstances are unparalleled.

Cap: The prostitute wears a flat ribbon knotted onto her hair rather than the more respectable cap.

Jewellery: A narrow row of very small pearls is worn around the neck.

Stockings: Blue silk with scarlet zigzags and a coronet above the scarlet gore clock, similar to those in Fig. 32; the garters are scarlet to match the decoration.

Shoes: Pointed, up-curving toes with high heels, the buckles unfastened over the high, cupid's-bow tongue; the front of the shoe is decorated with applied silver lace.

34. Women's shoes, 1730-1750

Blue/green silk damask, edged with green silk ribbon; a wide band of woven silver braid is applied to the front. The heels are covered with pink damask.

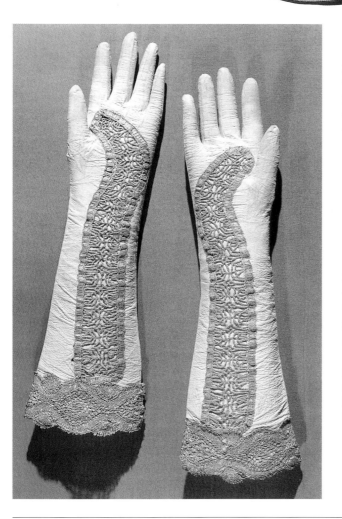

35. Women's gloves, 1735

White glazed-leather elbow-length gloves with an insertion of silver crochet work on the underside; edged with silver lace.

Note: This pair of gloves was worn by a bride in 1735. Other examples of this style have contrasting decoration in green and in black silk. The open-work effect can also be seen on the underside of surviving women's mittens of this period.

36. Fan, Dutch, 1735-1745

Paper leaf painted in polychrome gouache depicting a conversation piece in a garden setting; the reverse design is of a landscape. The pierced and carved ivory sticks are decorated with floral designs in various colours and there are small putti at the top of the guards.

Eighteenth-century accessories

37. Marriage à la Mode, Plate 2, Shortly after marriage, William Hogarth, 1743

Note: The young couple are already tiring of each other and spending far too much money. The disarray in their fashionable home after an evening of cards and music, also mirrors the disharmony of their marriage.

Headwear: The wife wears the modest white frilled cap tied under the chin which was usual daytime wear for married women; her husband's cocked hat is trimmed with expensive metal braid and feathers.

Stockings: Only a glimpse of the wife's pale silk stockings can be seen. The husband's stockings are worn in the fashionable manner rolled back and held by garters over the bottom of the breeches; both are wrinkled and one is loose. In contrast, the steward's dark practical stockings are smooth and worn in the less fashionable manner, held under the kneeband of the breeches.

Shoes: The high-heeled silk mules (see Fig. 31) worn by the wife are an elegant and fashionable indoor alternative to shoes. Men's footwear in the eighteenth century was simple, usually of dark leather with a plain or ornamented buckle. Fashions in buckles were often more innovative than in shoes. The husband's shoes have a rounded, upward-tilted toe and red heels, the latter denoted formal wear. The steward's shoes are sturdy, old-fashioned and practical with low heels and a square toe.

38. Men's shoes, 1736

White leather; the toes curve sharply upwards in the newly fashionable manner, and the flared heels are covered in red leather. The buckles are of silver set with paste.

Note: These shoes were made for the funeral effigy of the 2nd Duke of Buckingham after his early death at the age of nineteen. Shoes replaced boots except for riding and country wear in the early part of the eighteenth century and were, most usually, of black or dark brown leather. Red heels were worn at court and on the most formal occasions.

39. Shoe buckles, mid-eighteenth century

Silver and silver gilt metal set with paste and held by steel chapes (or clasps).

Note: Buckles came in oval, rectangular and square designs. They could be plain metal or elaborately decorated, using clear or coloured stones, precious, semi-precious and paste. They were worn on both men's and women's shoes. In addition, buckle makers provided smaller buckles to fasten breeches and, later, cravats.

40. Trade card of John Flude, mid-eighteenth century

This depicts the thriving trade in pawnbroking and the sale of second-hand clothes, jewellery and small domestic items such as candlesticks. The angled lower windows indicate the importance of buckles: many pairs are for sale.

Eighteenth-century accessories

Wardrobes bought in Town & Country.

BY JOHN FLUDE

Unredeemd Goods sold Wholesale & Retail.

Money Lent

Delegal sculp.t Bishopsgate.

John Flude

PAWNBROKER *and* **SILVERSMITH**

N.º 2 Grace Church Street

London.

Lends Money on Plate, Watches, Jewells, & Wearing Apparel, Houshold Goods, & Stock in Trade.

NB

Goods Sent from any Part of y.º Country directed as above, shall be duly attended too & the Utmost Value lent thereon.

LXXI

41. Fan, English, 1749

Engraved paper fan leaf with coloured washes. The bone sticks and guard have painted decoration in pink and blue on a sponged sea-green ground.

Note: Souvenir or commemorative fans were produced to mark significant occasions. This fan depicts the display of fireworks held in Green Park on 27 April 1749 to mark the peace of Aix-la-Chapelle which ended the War of Austrian Succession in 1748.

42. Trade bill, 1751/52

Although the design and principal wording suggests a 'Fan Ware-House', other goods supplied by Bar, Fisher & Sister included lace and millinery. A fan mending and remounting service was offered; both would be important because fans were an essential accessory for fashionable women.

At Gordon's Old Fan Ware-House,
the Golden Fan & Crown in Tavistock ſtreet,
Covent Garden,
LONDON.
is to be Sold all Manner of Fans Wholesale & Retail.
Likewiſe Lace, Childbed Linnen & all kinds of Millinary.
Lace join'd & mended, Fans Mounted, mended &c. by
Bar: Fisher & Sister, from Moore's lace-Chambers in Dukes Court

1751 Octr. 30th	Mrs Hucks Bt. of Bar: Fisher & Sister		
	a Rich Figur'd Sattin Capucheen flounced wth ye Same & lind wt Pink	1	13	0
1752	a Do. Do.	1	13	0
Febry. 12th	2 Bugle Necklaces	3	6	0
			2	0
		3	8	0

Febry. 12th 1752 Reced the Contents
in full of all Demands   Fisher

43. Engraving from Lewis's Islington, volume VIII, 1750s

This depiction of possible caricature heads is included to indicate the wide range of styles of cap, hat and jewellery for women, according to social position, wealth and age, and the types of wig and hat or cap worn by men according to age, means and occupation.

Eighteenth-century accessories

**44. The 1st Marquess of Downshire and his family,
Arthur Devis, c. 1755-1757**

Note: Before becoming the 1st Marquess of Downshire, Willis Hill (1718-1793) was Earl of Hillsborough and this painting is inscribed with the family's style of that period of their lives. This is a typical example of the English desire to be identified with rural pursuits and is, therefore, set within their country estate. The style of dress is relatively formal, and could have been worn in town.

Hats: Lady Downshire is wearing a small cap with a wired front which fits snugly over her head but is not likely to be flattened by the silk-covered straw hat held in her lap. Such hats protected the complexion from the sun and ensured that undesirable freckles or bronzing would not appear. The marquess is wearing a cocked hat. This style emerged at the end of the seventeenth century when the brim was turned up on three sides around a stiff, rounded crown into a neat triangle. It was universally popular throughout the eighteenth century and often edged, as in this example, with a metal lace. There were variations in style and this one is a Kevenhuller which featured a front which projected sharply forward.

Jewellery: Lady Downshire wears pearl earrings and a lace neck band. The marquess's breeches and shoes are fastened with metal buckles.

Gloves: Both Lady Downshire and her small daughter wear white, elbow-length mittens; the flaps of the former's pair are turned back to reveal a blue silk lining which matches her dress. Mittens were a popular lightweight alternative to gloves for women, freeing their fingers for embroidery and other domestic arts.

Stockings: The marquess is wearing white silk stockings which became increasingly fashionable for both sexes on formal or semi-formal occasions from the 1730s onwards.

Shoes: The narrow points of the girl's shoe and her mother's are just visible; the boy appears to be wearing a similar style. The marquess wears the black leather buckled shoe with high fronts and low heels, which was usual for men except in specific situations.

45. Woman's hat, c. 1750-1760

Vellum, covered on both sides with beige silk, the three layers stamped through with a pattern designed to simulate open-work lace. A single streamer of cream silk ribbon is at the centre back and there are long ties of white netted cotton.

Note: The shepherdess hat emerged in the 1730s and remained fashionable for informal wear until the 1770s. It was usually worn over white caps; the ribbon ties were left loose or used as a carrying handle. Such hats were worn in the garden (Fig. 44) and foreign visitors considered them an English style. Variations allowed the crown and brim to assume different dimensions and shapes. They were made from chip or willow straw covered with silk taffeta; or vellum, horsehair and

paper embossed to imitate straw. The crowns could be decorated with loops of ribbon. A particularly fine collection was preserved at Culver House, Exeter until sold at auction in the early 1980s. Examples of these included stiffened silk ribbon in chinoiserie style and feathers on a cotton base, lined with silk.

46. Man's hat, 1730-40

Black felted wool edged with silver lace and trimmed with white ostrich feathers. Its original box has the label of Chapman and Moore, 30 Old Street, London.

Note: This fashionable three-cornered hat is similar to that worn by the husband in Fig. 37. The cocked hat worn by men throughout the eighteenth century varied in minor details of style but was usually made from wool felt, beaver felt or a mixture of beaver and rabbit fur known as a demi-castor. It was nearly always black with the brim edged with metal lace and a button and loop attached to the left cock. Gentlemen invariably wore or carried a hat but it was wig not hat styles which changed most frequently in this period.

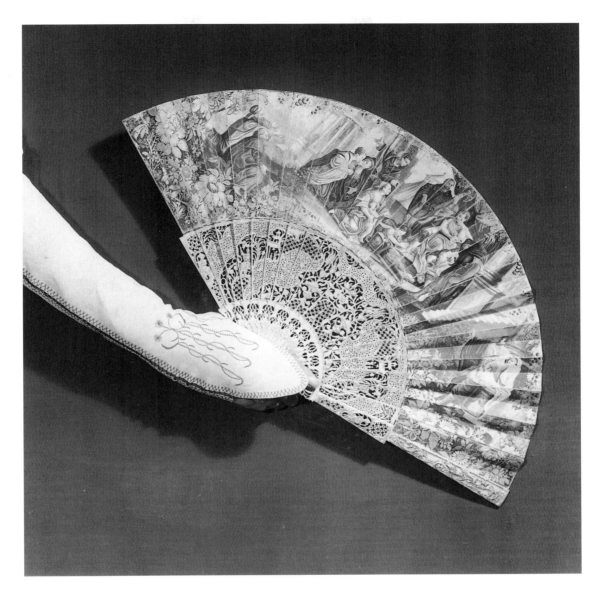

47. Woman's mitten and fan, 1720-1760

Elbow-length mitten of white linen seamed and embroidered with red silk, c. 1750-60. Fan with paper leaf painted in gouache depicting the Judgement of Solomon; carved and gilded ivory sticks and guards, c. 1720-60.

Note: Mittens were made from soft leather, silk or occasionally knitted silk and were usually elbow-length. Examples from the 1750s and 1760s often have a frill around the top edge which echoes the robings and decoration on bodices, skirts and petticoats at this date. Earlier eighteenth-century examples were often densely embroidered with naturalistic flower and leaf designs and those of leather could have a contrasting band of coloured silk under the curved flap which covered the fingers but was folded back for decorative and practical reasons (Fig. 44).

The decoration of fans mirrored changes in designs for silks and laces: the naturalistic floral motifs edging this leaf and the serpentine ribbon lace effect on the pierced sticks is similar to patterned silks of the mid- to late 1750s.

Eighteenth-century accessories

48. Lady Hertford, Antoine Roslin, 1765

Note: Lady Hertford's husband was the English ambassador to the court of Louis XV between 1763 and 1765; his wife is depicted in formal French court dress. Certain elements influenced the dress of other women throughout Europe.

Cap: Over her tightly curled and powdered hair, Lady Hertford wears a small black lace fly cap with a wired edge from which descends a pair of twisted lappets. The cap is adorned by a red silk pompon.

Jewellery: Pendant diamond earrings, a row of pearls just above the frilled 'necklace' of lace, a diamond bow necklet with slide and cross pendant and a set of graduated diamond stomacher brooches are the jewels of formal occasions. An English example of the lace 'necklace' can be seen in Reynolds's portrait of Susanna Beckford, 1756 (Tate Gallery, London). See colour plate IV.

Gloves: Lady Hertford wears one of a pair of long white silk gloves with the finger tips removed on her right hand, which loosely clasps the other glove.

Fan: A closed fan with ivory sticks; there is some indication of red in the design of the closed leaf.

49. Fan, French, 1775-1785

Fan leaf vellum with a central motif of lovers in a rustic setting with the symbols of Mars and Venus at either side and putti within oval medallions. Carved and pierced ivory sticks decorated with gold and silver leaf and spangles.

Note: The fan was a desirable female accessory throughout the eighteenth century and all European countries produced them in considerable numbers. These ranged from simple, inexpensive styles with bone sticks and paper leaves to highly ornate versions which used vellum, gold and silver leaf and other inlays.

50. Women's stockings, mid-eighteenth century

Left, blue silk with an embroidered flower motif in white, apricot, yellow and green silks. Middle, terracotta silk with stylized flower embroidery in white silk. Right, green silk with knitted white clock above which a flower and bird motif is embroidered in silver thread; white and terracotta stripes circle the top.

Note: A limited number survive of the many varieties of stocking produced and worn in the eighteenth century.
Technical innovations such as ribbing, knotting, lace clocks and the possibilities offered by silk, cotton and worsted suggest that both sexes had considerable choice.

51. Women's shoes, 1770-1785

Left, red leather bound with red silk; a narrow, medium-height heel extends as a wedge under the instep, 1770-80. Middle, pink satin brocaded with a floral motif in green, yellow and terracotta. The straps over the instep and the medium-height tapering heel are covered with pale green satin, 1775-85. Right, crimson damask bound with blue ribbon. The low fronts, without straps, are decorated with ruched striped satin ribbon of cream and green. The medium-height, tapering heels are covered with white leather, 1770-80.

52. Costume figure with parasol, 1775-1800

Note: Displays of costume in museums provide important three-dimensional information about the dress and accessories of a particular period. They are, however, rarely an accurate representation of what was actually worn. Museum curators work with the limitations of their collections, using items which might be typical or rare, of differing dates; frequently reproduction items are added, particularly gloves, stockings and shoes, which can be damaged by use on figures. Despite these difficulties, it is undoubtedly true that well-prepared costume figures provide a greater demonstration of a wide range of manufacturing and craft skills than almost any other display of comparable size.

Hat: The figure wears a shallow-brimmed straw hat tilted forward over the tall, full hairstyle of the mid- to late 1770s.

Scarf: The fine cotton gauze of the square kerchief with its delicate white embroidery is a forerunner of the buffon (see Fig. 54).

Parasol: Staff parasol of green silk, banded with white at the edge; cane stick with small bone hook and whalebone ribs, c. 1775-1800. The staff parasol (a later term) seems to have become fashionable around 1777 and remained popular until the early 1790s. Few such parasols survive but they do seem to have been amongst the first parasols to have been fashionable in England; the French had used them from early in the century. They had also reached America by the early 1770s, attracting considerable ridicule.

Shoes: These are reproduction but a style similar to those in Fig. 51 would be appropriate.

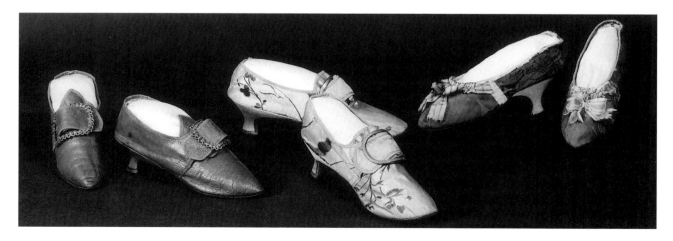

53. Woman's tie pockets, 1774

White corded linen embroidered in polychrome worsteds, mainly worked in chain stitch; the slits and edges bound with pink wool braid. Date and initials embroidered at the top of each pocket.

Note: Tie pockets, consisting of one, or more usually two flat fabric bags tied with a tape around the waist and reached by pocket holes in the sides of the skirt, were used in the seventeenth century. However those which survive in museum collections are mainly eighteenth century. They were often home-made and used silk, linen or cotton, but the most popular fabric was white dimity, a sturdy linen and cotton twill, strengthened with a canvas or buckram lining. They could be bought ready-made but many young women practised their embroidery skills on them and gave them as gifts. Such sturdy and capacious pockets contained all basic necessities; a New Englander bequeathed her pocket and its contents to a friend: the latter included a mirror, a hand-warmer and 'a strong-waters bottle' – presumably medicinal.

54. Buffon, c. 1780-1800

White cotton mull, approximately square with white cotton chain and knot stitch embroidery; when folded in a triangle the floral design on the back and front are in alignment.

Note: The fashionably full, rounded bosom of the 1780s was assisted by the careful arrangement of a buffon of the lightest muslin or silk gauze, often starched to maintain the desired outline. The young German, Sophie La Roche noticed 'Ladies with neckerchiefs puffed up so high their noses were scarcely visible' when she visited London in 1786.

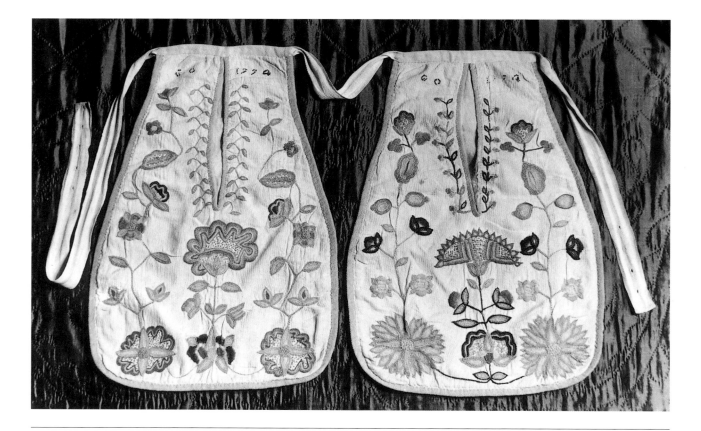

Eighteenth-century accessories

55. Wallet purse, c. 1780-1800

Green silk button-holed on a purse mould in a design of strawberries in red, brown and gold thread. The top is netted and the tassels are of silver thread; the sliders are missing. Probably home-made.

Note: Among amateur needlewomen in the eighteenth century, there was a great interest in open-work techniques like knotting and netting. One of the most popular types of purse to emerge in the post-1770 period was the long tubular wallet purse, known later as a 'miser', 'ring' or 'stocking' purse. This was a tube of fabric closed at each end with a horizontal slit in the middle of one side. Coins were pushed through the slit and allowed to fall to one or other end; the purse was carried at its middle. The silver or cut-steel rings or 'sliders' fitted around the middle; they could be moved towards each end to gather the fabric together and secure the contents. Early examples, like this one, were open-ended with just a single slider to close off the contents at the bottom. The double-ended version was the most popular and was still made for gaming counters as late as the 1920s. Netted purses could be bought ready-made but specialist shops catered for the needs of amateurs who often made them as gifts.

56. The Rev. D'Ewes Coke, his wife Hannah and Daniel Parker Coke MP, Joseph Wright of Derby, c. 1782

Note: Both men are wearing the country-style frock coat which, by this date, was increasingly acceptable wear for informal occasions in town also.

Jewellery: The full sash around Mrs Coke's waist is fastened with an oval buckle, possibly set with paste.

Scarf: A lightweight rectangular shawl of muslin or silk gauze embroidered with delicate motifs at each end is draped loosely over Mrs Coke's arms. A particularly fine example of these light, sinuous shawls is depicted in the double portrait by Gainsborough of Mr and Mrs Hallett, 'The Morning Walk' (National Gallery, London).

Umbrella: The short umbrella is green with a turned wood stick, brass ring and runner; the ribs do not appear to have added tips. Rather like the parasol, the umbrella took a long time to become acceptable in England, but from the 1770s onwards it gradually became a practical accessory for both sexes.

Eighteenth-century accessories

57. Umbrella, English, 1780-1800

Turned stick which is jointed and also unscrews into two parts; nine hinged whalebone ribs, green silk cover. The cord prevented the umbrella turning inside out in high winds. The runner is inscribed 'Hodges, No. 14 John Street, Adelphi'; this is probably the owner's name as the Adelphi was a fashionable London housing development, designed by Robert Adam.

Note: The philanthropist and traveller Jonas Hanway (1712-86) started to carry an umbrella when walking in London around 1750. At this date umbrellas were uncommon and Hanway's was a foreign one, possibly French, of the folding variety advertised in 1715 (Fig. 28), and depicted in Diderot's *Encyclopédie* of 1763, and seen in the illustration here. Umbrellas tended to be associated with foreigners or to be despised as 'the sign of having no carriage'. Gradually, opinion changed, they were imported from abroad and, by 1787, were being advertised of English manufacture. They were advertised in Boston in 1768, so their practical use was acknowledged in two continents.

58. Letter case or pocket book, 1780-1800

Paper covered with white silk crepe, embroidered with laid cord, pink silk ribbons and tamboured spangles. The central medallion of white satin contains a drawing of a classical urn.

Note: Many eighteenth-century pocket books were made in leathers such as shagreen or coloured morocco with note books of fine paper, vellum or ivory leaf; they are shown with spring catch fastenings on the trade cards of the 1720s and 1730s; as men's clothes became close-fitting many jewellers and stationers made suitably slim cases containing equipment such as knives, tweezers, earpicks, toothpicks, etc. Other cases were made of silk and, towards the end of the century, rather in the style of modern wallets with two compartments on each side opening towards the centre, the division between the two extending and folding back as a scalloped flap over the top compartment. Some were fitted out like the leather ones, but many were home-made. In the 1780s the *Lady's Magazine* issued several patterns for embroidered pocket books.

59. Fan, English, 1783

Printed paper decorated with coloured
washes and silver spangles; bone (?) sticks.
The central medallion commemorates the ascent
of the unmanned balloon of Messrs Charles and
Roberts in Paris on 27 August 1783. The side
medallions may record the flight of Michael Biaggini's
unmanned balloon, released from the Artillery Ground,
Moorfields, London on 25 November 1783.

Note: Ballooning caught the popular imagination in the 1780s and
commemorative prints, textiles and accessories reflected this
enthusiasm. There was also a 'balloon hat' for women; it had a
large balloon-shaped crown and wide brim and was usually made
from light silk or gauze held over a wire or chip foundation.

60. Beadwork purse, French, c. 1783-1784

Four triangular panels of multi-coloured sablé beadwork, lined with pink silk. Plaited silk drawstrings with beaded acorn tassels. The design depicts the balloonist Pilâtre de Rozier in the two-manned balloon in which he made his flight in November 1783.

Note: Although many varieties of purse were made in the eighteenth century, including framed purses using the new types of alloy which simulated gold (known in England as pinchbeck after its inventor), drawstring purses remained popular. Of the professionally made ones, the French sablé-beaded examples are particularly fine and were probably the work of specialist Parisian workshops. The term sablé means 'laid or covered with sand' and the beads were so minute that as many as one thousand per square inch might be used. Despite this, fairly complicated designs were a feature of these purses.

61. Fragment of a Kashmir shawl, eighteenth century

The motif shown here, the spade design, was very distinctive of real kashmirs and was later imitated at Paisley.

Note: It is difficult to give a precise date at which the fashion for Kashmir shawls began in England. However a letter of April 1777 reported that 'The shawls all come from Cassemire . . . [their] material the produce of a Thibet sheep.' Another popular motif was the buta, literally flower, described in the west as the cone or pine. Although some French Jouy cottons as early as 1766 apparently used the cone motif, French women recipients of genuine Indian kashmirs in 1788 cut them up to use for petticoats. Eventually, when they were worn as shawls in 1790 they were described as 'an English fashion'. Despite the difficulties of emulating the wool fabric and differences in technique, the English were attempting to manufacture woven shawls akin to kashmirs in Norwich (from the mid-1780s) and in Edinburgh at around the same time; printed shawls produced at Leven Printfield were mentioned by the *Glasgow Herald* in 1785. Depictions of their use are difficult to find before 1790 and silk scarves and shawls were more usual.

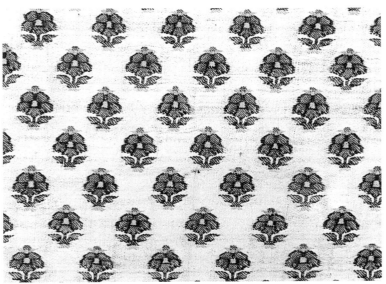

62. Such Things Are, engraving, 1787

Note: Throughout the eighteenth century and beyond, the absurdities of fashion provided ample subject matter for caricatures. Young men were a favourite target and this example dissects the details of extremes of fashion.

Hats: In addition to four variants of the excessively full, powdered wigs of the late 1780s, two methods of wearing a chapeau bras are depicted; with the points at back and front, or, as Napoleon always wore it, flat across the brow. One figure carries a cocked hat under his arm, and it is evident why carrying a chapeau bras will be less cumbersome.

Stockings: Stripes had been worn by fashionable young men in the 1770s and became popular again in the late 1780s (Fig. 65).

Footwear: Plain, flat shoes without buckles but fastened by ties suited the narrow, elongated lines of men's dress from the 1780s, but were a disaster for specialist buckle makers whose business shrank rapidly. Half-boots with a dip at the front were particularly popular in the 1790s.

Other: Tall walking sticks and large muffs were often ridiculed, but they are unlikely to have been used by more than a few young men.

Eighteenth-century accessories

63. Chapeau bras, c. 1796

Black felted wool, edged with black satin ribbon with an ornamental double cockade of ruched black ribbon. The inside of this hat bears the stamp which recorded payment of the hat tax. This tax was first introduced in 1783 but amended in 1796, substituting a stamp on the lining as proof of payment in place of a paper label.

Note: This style of hat became popular for formal dress wear in the 1780s. It was cocked at the back and front only, forming a half-circle, and could be easily carried under the arm. When worn it was usual for the two points to be at the back and front of the head, but its most famous wearer, Napoleon Bonaparte (from 1804 Emperor Napoleon I of France) resolutely wore it flat over the face with the points over the ears.

64. Men's gloves, c. 1795-1810

The top glove is one of a pair made of white cotton with a narrow turnover cuff, the embroidery in green silk and gold spangles. The lower glove is from a pair of machine-knitted silk with a broad navy stripe and a white stripe with a thin line of pink in the centre of the white; the pointing on the back of the hand is worked in pink silk.

Note: The size and style of these gloves suggest that they were for men. The cotton pair might have been worn for a semi-formal occasion, but the striped pair, like the stockings (Fig. 65) are ephemeral and flamboyant accessories, perhaps for a 'Jessamy', the 1790s successor to the Macaroni.

65. Stocking, 1790-1800

Silk, warp-frame knitted stocking, the zigzag pattern is worked in red, green, black, blue and yellow.

Note: Occasionally zigzag stripes are seen on men's stockings in prints and paintings, e.g. Vernet's *Les Incroyables* (1797), but plain stripes appear more often, especially in caricatures of Macaroni dress in the 1770s. Banded or horizontally striped hose were popular in the 1790s. All of these effects were made possible by a series of experiments and technical advances in the stocking frame industry from the 1770s onwards.

66. Fashion plate from Heideloff's Gallery of Fashion, 1794

Note: Nicklaus Wilhelm von Heideloff (1761-1839) came to England from France at the height of the Terror during the French Revolution and, in the *Gallery of Fashion* published between 1794 and 1802, produced a major series of illustrations of the latest fashions. Whether some or all of these were adopted by English women is uncertain but, to judge by the work of contemporary caricaturists, the English continued to live up to their earlier reputation of being overly fashionable at the expense of elegance.

Hats and caps: By 1792 the exuberance in hairstyles which had characterized the 1780s was over. Hair was dressed more closely to the head. Tall, crowned, narrow-brimmed hats and small helmet-shaped hats were popular, but close-fitting silk caps, especially turbans, were worn with every type of half- and full-dress toilette. These were invariably trimmed with nodding ostrich plumes and ruched ribbons.

Jewellery: The flat disc-like necklaces worn by the young women, from which pendants could be suspended, suggest the type of neo-classical jewellery of cameos, carnelians and similar semi-precious stones cut with classical motifs and set into delicate filigree settings. The interest in the antique world had absorbed scholars and antiquaries for much of the century, but a fresh impetus was added to its application to the decorative arts by the parallels drawn between revolutionary France, its quasi-democratic ideas, and the quasi-classical styles of dress adopted to reflect the new spirit of the age.

Tippets: These continued in the eighteenth century, less often made of fur, but as a light, twisted scarf of feathers, lace or, by 1780, 'plaited gauze'. However, with the appearance of the semi-classical chemise dress and the redingote and the higher waistlines of the 1790s, the tippet transformed itself into a 'snake' stole. These long fur or feather stoles could be loosely draped or knotted and are often depicted alongside feather plumes in caps and out-sized fur muffs. As all of these accessories contradicted rather than enhanced the increasingly stark neo-classical line being developed in France, they were short-lived fashions.

Gloves: These were worn up to or just beyond the elbow with ties to ensure that they did not slip down the arm. A narrow frill at the elbow or light printed decoration (see Fig. 67) were used on pale suede and leather. Muffs could be made with an inner pocket in which a coin purse, pocket book, etc. might be concealed rather than in tie pockets which could mar the line of the narrower skirts.

67. Women's gloves, c. 1795-1805

One pair from each of four pairs of wrist-length white kid printed in black; the wrist of each is scalloped and serrated with a hole punched at the base of each scallop.

Note: Many pairs of these gloves survive in museum collections in England, America and Europe. Apparently produced in Barcelona in Spain around the turn of the century they use a repertoire of printed designs. These include small figures taken from Jacques Callot engravings, swirling lines, diamond patterns, 'antique' motifs in contrasting bands and figures taken from mythology or popular legend.

68. Stocking, 1790-1810

Cream silk with embroidered lace clock, marked 'C' below the welt.

Note: Stockings with lace clocks were particularly popular with women. Similar decoration can be seen on the women's stockings in Fig. 70. Frame-knitted gloves and mittens with open-work patterns made by manual transference of loops from one needle to another were imported from Spain early in the century. Hosiers looking for novelties experimented with making open-work fabrics in the 1760s; this led to lace clocks and then to machine-made lace. Plain and lace clocks could also be embroidered on a smaller scale and in a manner more closely related to the stitches of the stocking using a technique called 'chevening', introduced in 1783. The colour could be contrasting or matching; silk was used on silk and wool stockings, and glazed linen on cotton stockings.

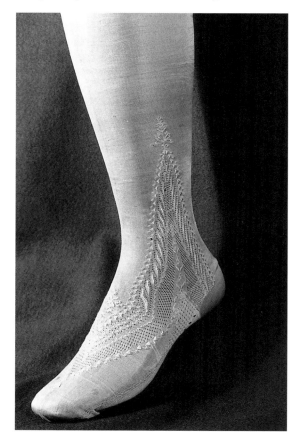

Eighteenth-century accessories

69. Women's shoes, c. 1785-1795

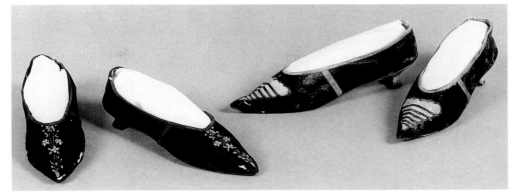

Left, black suede bound with green ribbon, the low fronts decorated with ribbon embroidery. The low heels taper to a narrow base and are covered with green leather. Right, black kid, the low fronts trimmed with pink kid insertions. The medium heels taper to a very narrow base and are covered with pink kid.

Note: Increasing numbers of women's shoes were made of kid leathers from the 1790s onwards. Styles varied considerably in regard to the shape of the toe, height and construction of heel, and the range of colours increased, allowing gloves and shoes to match, and also with shoes and stockings complementing each other; for instance pink stockings might have been worn with the shoes with the 'sandal-effect' pink kid insertions.

70. Eccentricities, Monstrosities, or Belles and Beaus of 1799, Isaac Cruikshank, 1799

Note: The swiftly changing styles of the last decade of the eighteenth century produced caricatures in almost the same quantity as fashion illustrations. The butt of this satire could be an individual (prince, politician) or a group apparently acting improperly or, a perennial favourite, the absurdities of the fashionable world.

Hats: All of the men are wearing, in embryonic form, the style known in the nineteenth century as a top hat. This had developed from the round hat: its crown rose much higher in the 1790s and at the end of the decade the brim grew smaller and the sides were rolled towards the crown. By this date all men of fashion had abandoned the powdered wig except for court wear and had short, tightly curled hairstyles and were growing side-whiskers. The women are wearing a novelty which appeared in 1799 called a 'poking' hat or bonnet. It was described as having 'a long projection like the beak of a snipe'. It bears some resemblance to a modern peaked cap, with a round section fitting closely on the head, an extended peak, the whole decorated with flowers, braids, ribbons, etc.

Jewellery: The young women wear rows of beads, perhaps pearls. In the foreground, the young man has a fob ribbon attached to a watch in the fob pocket in his pantaloons; from the ribbon would be suspended his personal seals and watch key.

Gloves: Both women wear the above-the-elbow gloves which were to stay in fashion for the next twenty years; the wrinkled appearance of these gloves might indicate that they are cut and stitched from linen or cotton rather than of suede.

Parasols: This is the first depiction of the small parasol with a 'marquise' hinge, so that it could be tilted vertically. The name 'marquise' was used later; it possibly refers to the Marquise de Pompadour (1721-1764), mistress of Louis XV, and an important arbiter of taste at the French court.

Stockings: The semi-transparent quality of the women's dresses enables us to see their garters, just above the knee. The patterning on the foot of the stockings suggests that these are of silk with lace clocks, made by framework knitters from 1783 and particularly popular with women (Fig. 68).

Shoes and boots: The women are wearing the low-heeled kid leather shoes of the late 1790s, often made in pale colours to match the light dresses or coloured stitching on their stockings. A small frill or bow decorates the front of the vamp. All but one of the men are wearing 'Hessians' - riding boots, calf-length behind and curving up to a point at the front from which is suspended a tassel. Usually of black leather with a narrow, coloured, top binding, they first appeared in England c. 1793/94. This caricature exaggerates the high front peak and transforms the tassels into small bells.

Pubd July 1st 1799
by SW Fores 50 Piccadilly

ECCENTRICITIES, MONSTRO

ITIES, or *Bell's* and *Beau's* of 1799.

Folios of Caracatures lent out for the Evening

71. Woman's parasol, 1800-1810

Green silk cover on whalebone ribs with folding stick and marquise hinge.

Note: This is very similar to the parasols that are depicted in Fig. 70. Most surviving examples of this type have turned wood sticks and green silk covers. From 1807 onwards the stick is quite plain and somewhat longer. This type of parasol is sometimes called a fan parasol because of a resemblance to the cockade fan.

72. Purse, French, 1800-1820

Pale-blue silk and silver thread worked in spider's-web pattern and decorated with a tassel of cut-steel beads. The silver frame is decorated with flower urns and sphinxes' heads, the latter motif became fashionable after Napoleon Bonaparte's expedition to Egypt in 1798.

Note: Most purses continued to be home-made in the first half of the nineteenth century and netting remained popular, the most usual type being a cobweb fine version of the wallet purse (Fig. 55). However, others, like this example were simple tubular bags weighted by a tassel and mounted on a press-button metal frame (or fastened by a drawstring). The introduction of the tiny gold sovereign in 1816 inspired the production of round sovereign purses mounted on curved metal frames, either netted or crocheted and measuring a mere 3 cm in diameter.

Nineteenth-century accessories

73. Lady Elgin, François Gérard, 1803

Note: The French fashions of the early nineteenth century were a combination of simplicity of line, for both men and women, with a use of restrained decoration; the accessories and fashions appeared harmonious and elegant. Lady Elgin wears a high-waisted velvet dress with applied gold decoration, for although thin cottons are associated with this period, silks and velvets were worn, particularly in winter. Lady Elgin wrote to her mother that her portrait 'was done by the best painter here and he took unconscious pains about it'. He certainly ensured that her portrait would compare favourably with those of her French contemporaries.

Jewellery: In her hair she wears a shallow tiara or comb edged with pearls to harmonise with her pendant pearl earrings. Around her neck is a double strand of chains with cameos with a lower half chain with a jewelled pendant suspended below the central cameo. The neo-classicism of this period is well reflected in its jewellery which used cameos, intaglios (and good imitations in shell, glass, lava and ceramic) set in gold held by delicate chains. Classical motifs such as Greek fret, ears of wheat, laurel vine leaves and grapes were used and all of these found expression in metalwork and semi-precious and precious stones.

74. Earrings, French, c. 1805

Gold plaques enamelled with classical heads set into half-pearl and red enamel borders; the bows are of woven gold wire.

Note: These form part of a rare parure of necklace, earrings and a pair of armlets from the French Empire period.

75. Portrait of an Unknown Woman, Henry-François Mulard, c. 1810

Note: This portrait, some five or seven years later than that of Lady Elgin (Fig. 73) does depict the pale, gauzy cottons so typical of the fluid, high-waisted dresses of the early years of the nineteenth century. It also suggests how this fashion might be moved from neo-classical severity to romantic prettiness by the addition of certain accessories.

Jewellery: On the head is the flatter bandeau or Greek fillet style of tiara or diadem which was reintroduced for both formal and semi-formal occasions. Around the neck is a row of coral beads from which a pendant (perhaps a cameo) is suspended.

Scarves, sashes and shawls: A Scottish plaid silk scarf with a fringed edge is loosely knotted below the collar and held in place by a striped silk sash. The pale wool shawl is probably French rather than Indian as it lacks the cone motif and the flower motifs are naturalistic rather than stylized; its short regular fringe has a machine-made look.

76. Woman's hat, 1812

Plaited dark brown silk rouleaux combined with netted silk cord and silk ribbon, both in a matching shade.

Note: By the close of the eighteenth century, all of the distinguishing features of millinery in the nineteenth and twentieth centuries had emerged. There was great seasonal change and variety, frivolity and wit in the use of trimmings. The hat was an essential accessory contributing to a new ideal of romantic femininity. To illustrate all the variants would be impossible. This hat, probably for evening wear, is in line with the taste for classicism. The use of the netting and the tiered tiara effect pays homage to Grecian antiquity, though this kind of sophisticated confection was unheard of at that time.

77. Woman's reticule, 1819-30

Beige watered silk with steel hoops and cut steel button. It is fastened at the top with a steel key which turns in a slot.

Note: The ingenuity and wit of early reticules easily matches the imaginative styles of millinery of similar date.

78. Woman's fan, English, c. 1810-1820

Pierced bone fan with polychrome flowers painted on one side and blue flowers only on the reverse, matching the ribbon threaded through the top.

Note: Intricately carved ivory fans had been imported from China throughout the eighteenth century. In the West skills developed in the comb-making industry were used to produce simpler and cheaper copies in bone and horn with decorative painted, spangle or gold-leaf effects.

Nineteenth-century accessories

Drawn Etch.d & Pub.d by Richard Dighton.May 1817.

Plate 2.d

A View from Knightsbridge Barracks.

Hat: Captain Seymour wears the black top hat worn by all gentlemen at this date. It has a very shallow brim and the crown is the same diameter throughout.

Gloves: For townwear, York tan gloves (a light yellow-brown sturdy leather) were appropriate with the increasingly subdued colours of daytime clothing – Captain Seymour's coat is brown and his trousers grey.

Umbrella: Green with easily visible brass spike and rib tips and the end of what appears to be a long runner. By this date the umbrella was as indispensable an accessory for men as the 'indispensable' (reticule) was for women. Umbrellas were even seen in warfare during rain at the siege of Bayonne (1813) in the Peninsular War; they were disapproved by Wellington as being ridiculous in this context. Umbrellas of this period had cane or whalebone ribs with brass tips, steel stretchers with pitchfork ends, often varnished or pickled to look like brass; a wood or metal stick, often with a brass conical ferrule (sometimes with a ball at the end) and a wood and ivory, antler or walrus-tusk cross handle. The cover, silk in best quality or cotton for cheaper versions, was usually green but could be blue, red or brown.

Boots: Black leather but without spurs; their top edge appears to reach to just below the knee; they are probably 'Wellington' boots.

79. A View from Knightsbridge Barracks, Richard Dighton, 1817

Note: Dighton, who came from a noted family of English artists, produced a series of caricatures of well-known London characters between 1816 and 1825. They were issued separately and in two collections, *West End Characters* and *City Characters*. This example, from the West End collection, depicts Captain Horace Seymour, a fashionable soldier, dressed for walking in town.

80. Men's clothing and accessories, 1795-1840

Note: This group of costume items was assembled to indicate some of the many fashionable styles and items available to wealthy and fashionable men. The double-breasted dressing gown dates from about 1825 to 1830 but is made from a Spitalfields silk brocade, c. 1765. The linen shirt dates from c. 1800 and the waistcoat of c. 1795 has fronts and collar made of Spitalfields silk satin.

Gloves: Ivory suede, c. 1825-1840.

Umbrella: Green silk with matching cover case and a bamboo handle, c. 1830- 1840. Owned by the 1st Duke of Wellington.

Stockings: Fine black silk woven with the initials GR at the top of each leg, c. 1820-1830. These belonged to George IV.

Footwear: The flat mules of cloth of silver lined with pink taffeta were made for George IV; a similar pair of cloth of gold also survive, c. 1820-1830. The boots are of black patent leather with a black Morocco leather leg, and have a shallow inner top lining of crimson Morocco leather, c. 1840. They were worn by the Duke of Wellington with a uniform.

81. Costume figure with tulle shawl, c. 1820

Note: Although it is less usual now, principally because of conservation requirements, to photograph costume on people rather than display figures, the flexibility of the human body does allow greater understanding of the possibilities of dress and accessories. The evening dress is of spotted ivory tulle with satin decoration over a matching underdress. The narrow classical lines of the first decade of the century gradually became more ornamental with decorated hemlines, frilled and ruched bodices and exuberant accessories after c. 1810.

Shawl: Ivory tulle woven with a silk flower pattern. Lightweight shawls suited the delicacy of this type of evening dress.

**82. Premium, Par and Discount,
I. and G. Cruikshank, 1822**

Note: The Cruikshanks, like the Dightons, were noted for their skills as caricaturists although the work of the former had a sharper satirical edge. The various styles of dress depicted suggest different social classes, financial circumstances and aspirations. The young man to the left is a dandy whose major interest in life is fashionable clothing; the father and two daughters are probably comfortably middle class, the man's clothing would be worn by a clergyman or a City merchant at this date. The young man to the right is conventionally dressed in the manner of an aspirant clerk or visitor to town from the country.

Hats: Two styles of top hat are shown: the dandy's well-blocked and glossy top hat, tipped over one ear and revealing the teased side curls (possibly assisted by false hair) of the current fashion; and the young aspirant's older, slightly battered top hat which lacks the new height and crown-top width of the popular Wellington shape of the 1820s and 1830s. The father wears the wide-brimmed round hat, an unfashionable but practical felted wool, that retained favour with certain groups in society throughout the nineteenth century. The young women are wearing poke bonnets, a style which, with variants, lasted throughout the nineteenth century. Its open brim always projected forwards over the face and it was tied under the chin; it could be made of straw, silk or cotton, either fairly plain or decorated with flowers and ribbons.

Jewellery: The dandy has a glass, possibly set in decorative metalwork, on a long cord suspended around his neck under the shawl collar of his waistcoat. The watch key suspended from the other young man's fob ribbon can be seen swinging loosely at his waist.

Gloves: The dandy is carrying one glove, of a light, soft leather by this date; by the late 1820s yellow, pink, sky blue and lilac gloves were worn in daytime in addition to the traditional light tan and buff varieties.

Umbrellas: From left to right these fall into the categories of fashionable, family and everyday. All are large with only a short distance between the rib tips and the handle, and above the spike on the umbrella (right) is a protruding leather washer, a feature of many umbrellas in the first half of the nineteenth century.

Stockings: Those that can be seen are a plain white. The young man (right) wearing old-fashioned breeches has also put gaiters over his stockings and shoes to protect them. These were worn by both men and women and made in a variety of practical, that is, washable, and impractical (for female fashion use) fabrics.

Shoes and boots: The dandy wears fashionable Wellington boots under his pantaloons with, it is likely, detachable spurs. The others all wear plain, heel-less leather shoes fastened at the front.

83. Shawl border, English, c. 1825

Cream wool and silk shawl with polychrome design of
flowers, the border woven with the traditional 'cone'
motif. This is a Norwich shawl using the fillover
technique, so-called because 'in the weaving the face of
the shawl is downward, and all the work comprising the
figure is filled over it'. This may be taken to mean that
on the 'wrong' side, details of the pattern were obscured
or 'filled over' by floating wefts. Usually a silk warp was
used with a wool weft but even if the shawl was entirely
spun from silk the fillover was always wool.

Note: Norwich had a long tradition of textile manufacture before
Edward Barrow commenced manufacturing shawls there in 1784.
By 1802 there were twelve manufacturers, most still using hand
embroidery, but around this date the fillover technique was
invented. Edinburgh shawls vied with Norwich for delicacy of
colour and production of goods in the spirit of true Kashmirs, but
both gradually were overtaken by Paisley-manufactured shawls
later in the century.

84. Reticule, English, 1820-30

Bias-cut white silk taffeta gathered front and back to a medallion of stiffened card. The central motif is an imitation cameo of red and white wax surrounded by pheasant feathers. The top opening is trimmed with silk fringe and fastened with white silk ribbon drawstrings and bows.

Note: Circular bags seem to have been particularly popular in the 1820s. It was an easy style to make and allowed amateur needlewomen to match bags to shoes, hats and other accessories. The feathers on this example may suggest that it complemented a feather muff or tippet or echoed the feather decoration on a hat.

85. Umbrellas, 1820-1865

Left, thick bamboo handle, thin black-japanned stick, rectangular metal ribs, green silk cover edged with blue and pink band, 1840-50. Centre left, antler handle on cane stem, wood stick, brass spike, eight cane ribs with brass tips, shot green silk cover; runner marked 'Hobday, Francis and Co, Royal Letters Patent', 1821-32. Centre right, ivory or bone handle marked 'F. Lindner, Albion Road, Holloway' (the owner), cane stick and eight Paragon-type ribs with white tips. Brown cover, possibly alpaca. Marked 'Sangsters' on central reinforcement, 1860-65. Right, bone knob on painted wood stem, thick beech stick, nine whalebone ribs, brass tips and spike, green and blue shot silk cover banded at the edge with pink, 1820-30.

Note: The umbrella (left) is associated with the 1st Duke of Wellington and when closed slips into a silk cover and into two interlocking lengths of bamboo which slot together with the handle to form a bulky cane. The umbrella (centre left) includes improvements to the frame patented by Samuel Hobday of Birmingham in 1821. The umbrella (centre right) uses the U-section rib and stretcher, sold with special furniture under the trade name 'Paragon'. It was patented by Samuel Fox in 1852 and was hugely successful as it enabled him to make a slimmer umbrella. It is still produced, hardly modified, today. Umbrellas were used by both men and women, the latter's being somewhat smaller but otherwise fairly utilitarian. Fashions in umbrellas changed slowly, unlike parasols, and it was the technical advances which made it slimmer which marked this period. Silk, mainly green and brown and, from 1848, the cheaper alpaca (centre right) were usual.

MARINE COSTUME.

Published by G. B. Whittaker for La Belle Assemblée, No 20 new series July 1 1826.

86. 'Marine Costume'
Fashion plate, La Belle Assemblée, July 1826

Note: A number of fashionable seaside resorts attracted visitors from the late eighteenth century onwards. These included Brighton, popularized by George IV when a young man, Weymouth and Lyme Regis, the last visited by Anne Elliott in Jane Austen's *Persuasion*. Whether the styles of dress suggested for such summer visits were especially designed with considerations of sand, shingle and salt air in mind is doubtful.

Hat: White *gros de Naples* (a type of stout taffeta or corded silk) trimmed with lace and tulips and broad silk ties.

Jewellery: A row of pearls and pendant pearl earrings indicate the perennial attraction of these items. Around the left wrist, worn over the glove, is a close-fitting bracelet, a fashion more usually associated with the 1840s and 1850s.

Parasol: Green, probably silk, with turned wood handle and the small hook which is characteristic of the 1820s.

Neckwear: Wide, cape-like collar known as a pelerine, with scalloped edges and ribbon threaded through to match the skirt decoration.

Gloves: Short, plain, wrist-length worn tucked under the sleeve cuffs.

Reticule: Similar in design to the example illustrated in Fig. 90.

Stockings: White with no apparent sign of lace clocks.

Shoes: The low-heeled black French style which dominated female fashion from c. 1823 onwards.

87. Woman's bonnet, English, c. 1829-31

Cream taffeta drawn over wires trimmed with matching, ruched fabric.

Note: The exuberant millinery styles of the later 1820s and early 1830s had been signalled at the end of the Napoleonic wars when the English had renewed contact with French fashion. As early as 1815 tall crowned hats with upstanding ribbon bows and large artificial flowers were satirized as 'a chimney pot with a sweep's brush sticking out at the top'. In 1818 brims expanded dramatically to accommodate massed curls around the face, and between 1820 and 1825 homage was paid to Mary Stuart (the sixteenth-century Queen of Scotland) with brims similar, or wider, to those depicted in portraits of her. Wired brims and decorations stretched upwards and outwards at the height of this exuberance in 1827-1830 and the hat was tilted asymmetrically over fuller curls on the right of the face. Exotic new introductions to English gardens: hydrangeas, peonies and magnolia blossoms vied with plumes, ribbons and birds of paradise as decorations perched around and on top of the crown.

88. Olive green taffeta bonnet, c. 1830-35

High, inverted flowerpot style crown on wire and straw frame, deep wide brim, deep bavolet covered in black crêpe, self-fabric lining.

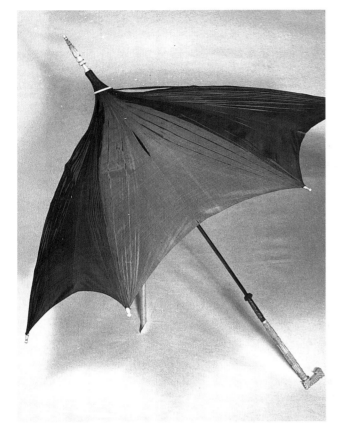

89. Woman's parasol, English, 1830-40

Carved ivory handle and ferrule, with ivory tips to the eight whalebone ribs, lacquered iron stretchers, brass stick, hinge cover embossed with a crown and 'London' above palm leaves, ring closure of ivory and green silk cover in pagoda shape.

Note: Parasols became an important accessory in the nineteenth century and, like all other accessories, were susceptible to changes in fashion: colour, trimming, shape and size varied considerably and manufacturers vied to produce both technical and aesthetic improvements. By 1809 the pagoda or 'Chinese' shape, forming an ogee or Tudor arch in profile had arrived and remained fashionable until the late 1830s. Parasols were large in the 1830s (approximately 38 inches long and 36 inches in diameter when open). Green remained a popular colour, the voters of Eatanowill in Charles Dickens' *The Posthumous Papers of the Pickwick Club* (published 1836/7) were bribed with 'five-and-forty green parasols, at seven and sixpence a-piece' for their wives.

90. Reticule, ?French, 1820-1830

Steel mesh trimmed with cut-steel paillettes and steel fringe. Top fastening by a loop which fits over a steel key; some examples have an attached lining with a drawstring top.

Note: By 1799 *The Times* was recording 'The total abjuration of the female pocket . . . Every fashionable fair carries her purse in her workbag.' Work bags, used for fashionable pursuits such as knotting were given longer strings and this 'new' accessory was illustrated in the *Gallery of Fashion*, November 1799 with the note 'Indispensables are bags, which the ladies use instead of pockets.' The new name 'indispensable' did not match the French name 'ridicule', but both mocked their owners. Eventually the French term 'reticule' came to dominate, but early in the nineteenth century they were known as indispensables and ridicules. Light frames and fabrics sufficed for these accessories which became highly inventive and decorative between 1800 and 1830. Like hats, bags had found a role and reflected both classical and romantic taste using silk, velvet, netted silk, beads and metalwork and, from c. 1815, leather.

91. Hair ornament or comb mount, English, 1830-1840

Gold wire and pressed sheet gold with carved carnelian, amethyst and garnet flowerheads and gold stamens; surrounded by groups of gold flowers set with a variety of coloured semi-precious gemstones and pearls. All mounted on a diadem-shaped frame of gold.

92. Fashion plate from The World of Fashion, January 1832

Note: The evolution of fashion plates and their changing content gives a fascinating glimpse into women's and, to a lesser extent, men's fashionable preoccupations. In the early 1830s women's hats, bonnets, hairstyles and hair decorations were a dominant feature. By this time, the counter-balancing shoulder width, which suited high and wide heads, was being matched by much fuller skirts as the waistline returned to a more natural level. This overblown rose effect was, to a degree, mitigated by the use of decorative surface effects and delicate accessories.

Hats: The asymmetrical nature of female headwear can be seen in the front and back views depicted. The shallow crowns and stiffened brims are buried beneath ruched ribbons, cockades and feathers, and the evening hairstyles include the 'Apollo knot' (right) festooned with wired flowers, either artificial or with a jewelled decoration (Fig. 91).

Jewellery: The woman in day dress (left) wears matching wide bracelets fitted close to the wrist and a wide ornamental buckle. The two women (right) have pendant earrings, possibly flowers, to complement their hair ornaments.

Shawl: Rectangular, possibly of silk, with a deep fringed border.

Gloves: Short, plain leather wrist-length gloves (left) and long, pale evening gloves at the fashionable below-elbow length (centre and right).

Stockings: The figure (left) wears stockings with a zigzag pattern and the one in the centre wears open-work striped with plain bands.

Shoes: The fashionable black leather or cloth flat-heeled shoe with ties over the foot and round the ankle is seen with daywear. The evening style is similar but made from pale satin with matching ribbons.

Newest Fashions for January 1832. Morning and Evening Dresses.

93. Women's gloves, 1825-40

Three gloves, each from pairs made of white kid embroidered with flower and leaf designs; the embroidery in gold or silver thread or polychrome silks.

Note: Once women's day dresses were invariably long-sleeved, gloves were usually wrist-length, except for evening wear; by the 1830s, mittens were popular alternatives. The decoration on both day and evening gloves and the fashionable materials were similar, light-coloured leather (usually kid) 'which can only be worn for one day', knitted gloves, silk net in pastel shades, white and for net mittens, black. Flower embroidery in a formal design or arranged in rows or scattered sprigs bore a similarity to the long-stemmed mobility of artificial flowers on hats and as executed in the jewellery of this date (Fig. 91). The glove trade, which should have benefited from the widespread wearing of gloves and the need to replace them frequently, was damaged by government action in 1825 which lifted the prohibition on foreign luxury goods. The market was soon flooded by cheaper German, Italian, Austrian and, most especially, French gloves. By 1832 over 1.5 million pairs of French gloves were imported into England. This precipitated the collapse of various glovemaking centres until surviving manufacturers adjusted to new circumstances by concentrating on certain types of production and by making agreements with French companies.

94. Stocking, English, 1832-35

Fine white cotton with embroidered open-work at the front of the foot; marked 'A . . . A' (for Allen, Solly and Allen).

Note: During the Napoleonic wars silk was scarce in England and manufacturers concentrated on providing a finer thread spun from Indian and Egyptian cottons. Various new processes ensured that Nottingham manufacturers led the way in the making of fine, smooth cotton stockings. In 1815 French women preferred fine India cotton stockings from England to silk hose from Paris and by 1822 open-work cotton stockings were generally worn unless the dress was of silk. The marking of stockings with initials worked into the knitting on or just below the welt was an identification mark for a firm's goods which began in the late eighteenth century, although the earliest worked stocking which is dated is one of 1826 in the J. R. Allen collection at Nottingham, England; it has 'A' for John Allen & Sons. Other types of earlier and later marks in England and elsewhere can be useful guides to dating, manufacture or ownership.

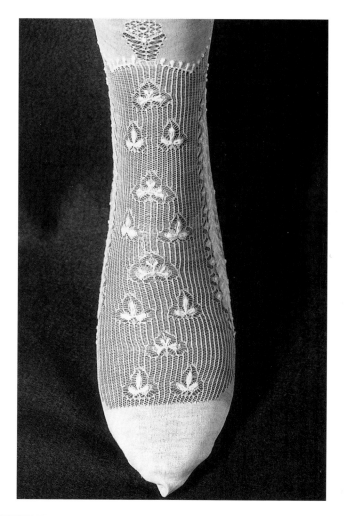

The Duchess of Kent. The Queen. Prince Albert.

The Latest & Newest London & Paris Fashions 1843. Morning & Evening Dresses.

95. Fashion plate, 1843

Note: Queen Victoria, Prince Albert and the Duchess of Kent are depicted wearing the latest fashions. This is an idealized group - the Queen was shorter and the Duchess was stouter.

Hat: The Duchess is wearing the close-fitting style of bonnet which became popular in the 1830s, and fitted close to the head over the sleek, flat hairstyles. For evenings, feathers and lace lappets added height and fullness.

Jewellery: The Prince has a prominent cravat stud and the Queen wears two matching pairs of bracelets.

Shawls: These could be narrow, rectangular scarf shawls or, as in the example draped over the piano, large, often square shawls; the latter hints at an Indian or 'Paisley' design in the deep border.

Muff: An attractive though somewhat impractical alternative to gloves; sometimes there was a small inside pocket to hold a handkerchief or coins.

Fan: The Queen holds a folded fan.

Socks: Once men generally wore pantaloons with a strap under the foot (as here) or trousers, there was no need for stockings except for formal evening wear with breeches. Half-hose or socks were worn. (Fig. 102).

Shoes: The Prince wears low-cut, flat-heeled black leather shoes, similar in construction to women's of this date but made of leather. Women often wore satin shoes in their homes.

96. Woman's bonnet, English, 1840-50

Black velvet with drab green figured silk ribbons and matching ties.

Note: Although the wide-shouldered sleeve continued in fashion until 1835 the reduction in the size of millinery had begun in 1832. The 'bibi' bonnet appeared with a small crown placed further back on the head and a brim which descended low at the ears but open across the forehead. By 1835 the brim reared up, off the face, framing it closely in a high oval while the narrow, tapering crown met it at an acute angle. By 1837 the bonnet brim developed a downward curve at the chin edge and two years later the brims met at the chin forming a complete, face-enclosing circle. By 1840 the close-fitting bonnet had ousted all other daytime styles and its crown and brim merged together in a single horizontal line. This move away from flamboyant display towards shrinking modesty was matched by a smoother, flatter hairstyle and the bonnet also acquired a bavolet (a modesty frill at the back of the neck) and, as indoor caps could not be worn under the new style, an inner edging of lace and artificial flowers within the brim.

97. Parure, English, c. 1850

Necklace, brooch and earrings of seed pearls strung onto open-work plaques of mother of pearl.

Note: Delicate, stylized flower and leaf designs were found on a number of accessories.

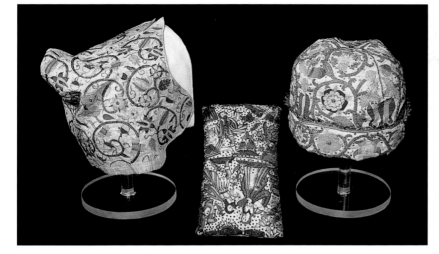

I. Caps, 1600-1620

Left, a woman's coif, right, a man's cap, both of linen embroidered with gold thread and polychrome silks; the cap is decorated with spangles. The scrolling design of stems and flower heads is typical of late sixteenth- and early seventeenth-century embroidery and is found also on gloves and drawstring bags. The small pillow is of slightly later date and embroidered with biblical scenes.

II. Boy's stockings, 1590-1610

Hand-knitted in silk with a regular design of gold and silver motifs; the tops are elaborately decorated suggesting that they were meant to be seen below the trunkhose or breeches. Such overall design is seen infrequently in portraits of the time, a motif or 'clock' at the ankle is more typical.

III. Parasol cover, Italian, 1660-1710

Ribbed silk edged with silk ribbon, embroidered with gold thread and polychrome silks. The elegant design of the embroidery suggests that the parasol may have been carried at an angle, possibly in the manner of the servant holding the Marchesa Elena Grimaldi's parasol in Van Dyck's portrait, c. 1623 (The National Gallery of Art, Washington).

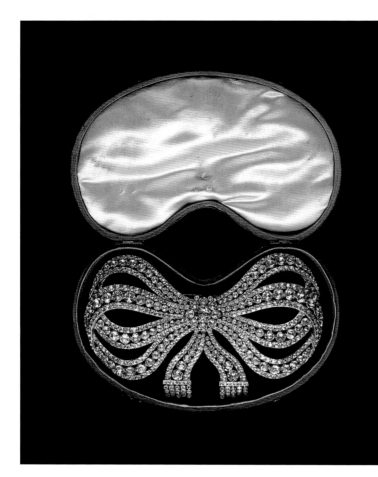

IV. Stomacher brooch, 1760-1770

Fine-quality pastes set in silver alloy; the jeweller's case is original and is made of paper treated to resemble sharkskin.

V. Woman's shoes, 1760-1770

Blue silk with applied silver lace and spangle decoration, the serpentine design is similar in style to the curving lines of the stomacher brooch. Maker's label of 'Francis Poole, Women's Shoemaker in the Old Change near Cheapside'. This is a rare survival of a London shoemaker's label from this period.

VI. Two pendants, 1780-1800

Right, gold with two glass compartments, the upper contains bows of hair and seed pearls, the lower is of painted ivory. The neo-classical plinth is set with gold wire and seed pearls. Left, gold frame set with seed pearls containing a monument on an ivory ground, the former decorated with diamonds, gold banding and swags set with seed pearls. A back compartment contains plaited hair. Such items of jewellery are associated with mourning.

VII. Tobacco pouch and purses, 1800-1900

A selection of the many styles, patterns and colours found on small purses in the nineteenth century. These include a drawstring tobacco pouch crocheted in silk, lined in kid, 1850-70 (top left); a crown purse of silk and metal mesh with gilt frame and chain to hold crown coins, 1880-1900 (second top left); a long purse of watered silk with vandyck points, gilt metal braid and trimmings, 1820-30 (centre row, top); and a netted silk with steel beads and trimmings, 1800-1810 (centre row, second from top).

VIII. Fan, Italian/French, 1828

Painted vellum leaf with a central view of the Colosseum in Rome. Guard sticks of mother-of-pearl overlaid with chased gold floral openwork. On each stick are three circular compartments containing hair under rock crystal, bordered with amethysts, garnets and emeralds.

IX. Shawl, 1843

Silk-warp and wool-weft twill with fillover tabby weave in wool; knotted silk fringe. This detail from a Norwich shawl has an almost Chinese quality to the design, and there was considerable fascination with Chinese designs and products in the mid-nineteenth century.

X. Shawl, 1844

Silk-warp and wool-weft twill with fillover of wool with some silk. The colour is known as 'Norwich Red', and the detail shown here displays part of the end border of this rectangular shawl. The sophisticated design twists the pine-cone design diagonally and intertwines it with foliage.

XI. Parasols, 1840-1850

Two Chinese export parasols. Left, ivory handle carved with flowers and leaves with a female figure as the ferrule. The silk cover is embroidered in silk threads and the faces of the figures are of ivory; the cover is lined with red silk. Right, ivory handle carved with pagodas and flowers. The satin cover was embroidered with English flowers to Queen Victoria's order.

XII. Necklace, 1870-1880

Narrow band of velvet hung with fourteen strings of French jet (black glass) faceted stones, each with a larger hexagonal pendant at the end. Such jewellery was often worn with mourning dress.

XIII. Women's stockings, 1870-1890

Silk, the two right-hand pairs date from c. 1870, the near left one is labelled 1881; the one to the left is from c. 1890.

XIV. Fans and gloves, 1828-1905

Top left, silk leaves painted with lily of the valley swags and bunches of roses, shamrocks and thistles; pierced mother of pearl sticks. The cypher of Queen Victoria and the date 24 May 1858 is on the central leaf. Right, silk leaf painted in gouache with irises; imitation amber sticks set with steel spangles, c. 1895. The closed fan is at plate VIII. The kid leather evening gloves are typical of late nineteenth- and early twentieth-century fashions.

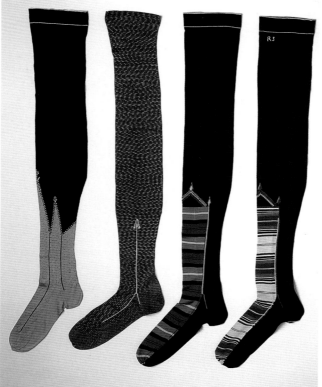

XV. Fans, 1900-1930

Paper fans advertising hotels, theatres, restaurants and so forth were often given as free gifts to patrons. The earliest example is from the Savoy (bottom left); to the right is a patriotic souvenir depicting leaders in the Boer War in South Africa (1899-1902).

XVI. Parasols, Belgian, 1923-1928

Left, horn handle carved as an owl; silk cover. Centre, ribbed ivory cap on a ribbed wooden handle, the silk georgette cover forms a flower when open. Right, wood pistol-butt handle and one-piece tussore cover printed with an Aztec-inspired design.

Next page: XVII. Poster advertising the collection of footwear at Northampton Museums and Art Gallery

This is an excellent illustration of the diversity and range of footwear which has survived over many centuries. It includes fashionable and functional items as well as examples from different countries. Public collections of one type of accessory are rare; Northampton has the largest collection of boots and shoes in the world. It provides a significant resource for students and scholars and is of great fascination to the general public.

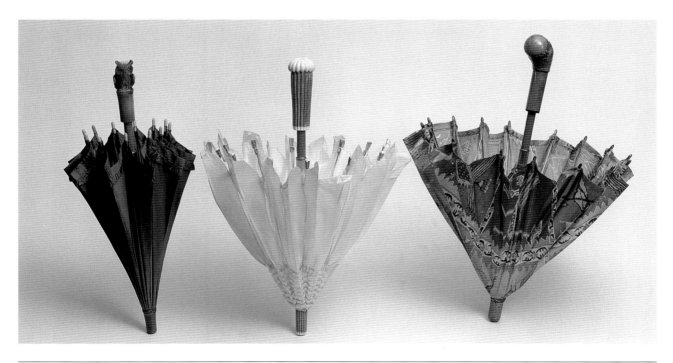

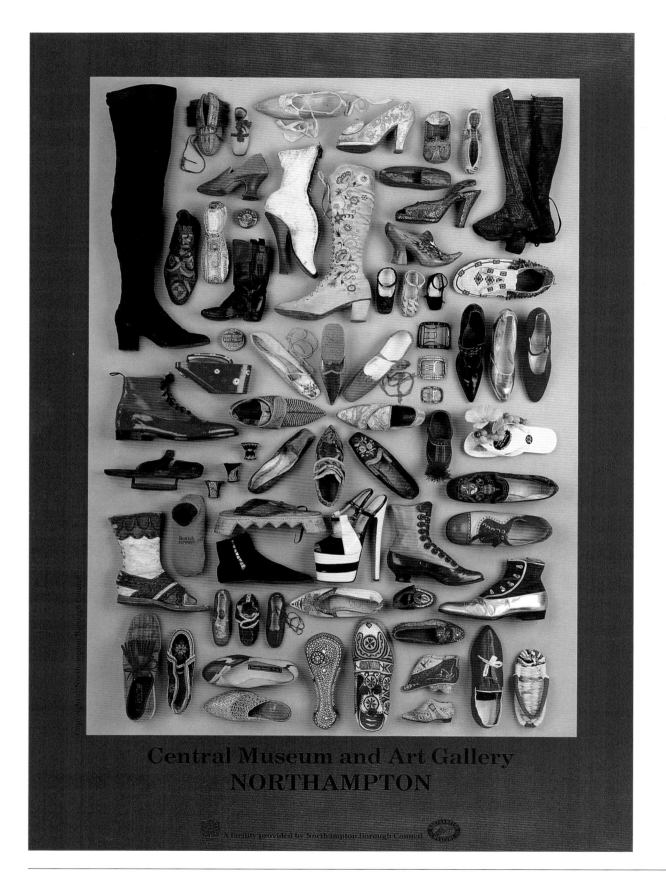

Central Museum and Art Gallery
NORTHAMPTON

A facility provided by Northampton Borough Council

The Visual History of Costume Accessories

98. Woman's shawl, English, 1840-60

White muslin with tambour-work diaper spots and inner border design of field flowers.

Note: Embroidered shawls enjoyed popularity for evening wear as did imitation lace shawls and scarves made on a Leavers lace machine. This shawl was produced at Coggeshall, Essex where a thriving cottage industry for tambour embroidery on net was established by a refugee called Monsieur Draygo, of French or Flemish extraction.

99. Women's mittens and a fan, 1840-45

Mittens: Black silk net embroidered in a flower design with beads, gold and silver thread and green and red silk.

Fan: Bone sticks and guards; paper leaf with a pastoral scene.

Note: Black net mittens, plain, open weave or with applied or embroidered decoration, were worn by the elderly or by ingenues as an acceptable alternative to gloves in the evening. Cream or white cotton or netted silk mittens were much favoured with day dress. From the mid-1840s onwards early forms of elastication (India rubber strands knitted into the fabric) ensured a closer fit around the wrist. Both day and evening wear gloves and mittens decreased to wrist length, or just above, from about 1840 until the mid-1860s.

100. Two parasols, English, 1844-50

Left, small ivory hook handle, carved ferrule, wood stick; cover of blue and pink shot silk woven in a chessboard pattern, knotted-on pink and blue fringe, white silk lining. The ribs are bent near the tips, possibly it opened automatically. The runner is marked 'Royal Windsor, Reg. 13th Feby 1844'. Right, ivory handle carved with a greyhound's head, brass joint cover, twelve solid steel 10-inch ribs, blue silk cover trimmed with Bedfordshire Maltese lace and knotted-on blue and white silk fringe. Runner marked 'Patent Stella, Regd. 30 Dec. 1850'. The ribs and the shape of the cover make a star (stella) shape.

Note: In 1838 carriage parasols became fashionable as open carriages became popular. The income and aspirations of a growing middle class provided a large market for all types of novelties for wear or in the home. Examination of

patented inventions indicates use of the new copyright laws (1839 and 1842) by, in particular, W. & J. Sangster of 140 Regent Street, London. The 'Royal Windsor' was one of their models, although the 'La Sylphide', also registered in 1844, proved especially popular and a number of these survive in museum collections. Novelty and exclusiveness were important to manufacturers but, in general, the parasols of the early 1840s are very plain with understated trimmings. Although a number of variations in the details can be found, green and brown continued as popular colours until the late 1840s when strong shades of pink and blue became fashionable. In 1842 the *Illustrated London News* recorded a feature of many 1840s' accessories, 'lace and embroidered borders continue to be favourite trimmings for dress. The former, indeed, is in high vogue - lace parasols, lace fans, lace shawls and lace mantles being everywhere the rage.' See colour plate XVI.

101. Fan, ?French, 1851

Printed paper with colour wash; the leaf depicts the Great Exhibition structure of glass and iron originally sited in Hyde Park, with flags of exhibiting nations to left and right. Bone sticks and guard.

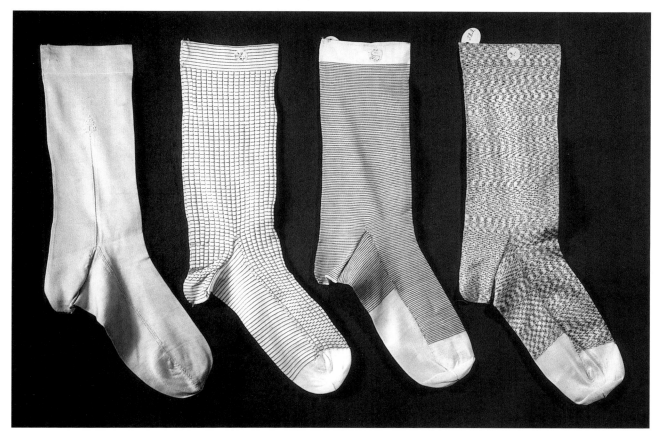

102. Men's socks, English. 1830-40

Left to right, pale-lilac silk with embroidered arrowhead clock; white silk with blue lines, the stripes made by taking out a needle every eighth stitch; white silk with lines space-dyed in blue and black; white silk, space-dyed in black.

Note: These examples and others were exhibited by Allen and Solly at the Great Exhibition in 1851. Once boots, pantaloons and then trousers came into fashion, the need for men's stockings for fashionable wear diminished to evening and formal occasions. This happened over a period of several decades during which half-hose, literally half-stockings with a welt at the top, were introduced. These were fine when worn under pantaloons which fitted the leg tightly, but under looser trousers a ribbed, supporting cuff was required. Precisely when this happened is difficult to pinpoint, but by October 1856 they appear on a pair of men's banded socks in a *Punch* cartoon.

The Great Exhibition was a major showcase for British manufacturers and included accesories (Figs. 102, 108), fabrics and clothing as well as many other classes of material.

103. The Empty Purse, James Collinson, 1857

Note: This painting is typical of the genre scenes which were admired by the Victorian public. It took an experience known to or observed by a large section of the educated population and translated it into a work of art. The almost photographic accuracy of the depiction of the details of this church bazaar may not be wholly unconscious; at this time the challenge posed by the new form of recording people and their circumstances was of interest and concern to conventional artists.

Hats: The young woman is wearing a bonnet approximating to the 'fanchon' style; the bonnet brim has retreated and its edge is marked by the close band of flowers while the loose chignon is taken into a pouched caul of fabric, the whole confection masked by the satin-edged, spotted tulle veil attached to the crown. The hat on display is a modified round hat (Fig. 104) with curled front brim and feather plume suitable for walking and riding.

Jewellery: A narrow, close-fitting bracelet is worn on the right wrist; technical advances ensured that a bracelet could be adjusted to fit an arm, wrist or, a little later, over a glove.

Gloves: Plain leather, tightly fitted to the wrist (see left palm, holding purse) by means of a button or snap-dome fastener introduced by M. Raymond of Grenoble, c. 1855.

Purse: A beaded 'wallet' or 'long' purse, the round end trimmed with a metal tassel and the straight end with a fringe; the young woman is holding one of the metal sliders in her right hand. Vast numbers of these purses were worked by Victorian women, using crochet or knitting, in silk or cotton thread and ornamented with gilt or steel beads. Having one end square and fringed allowed their users to place gold and silver coins at different ends and distinguish where they were placed. See colour plate VII.

Embroidery: The growing range of women's magazines produced ideas for knitting, embroidery and the production of novelties of which purses were an obvious example. Embroidered braces and slippers (top right and far left) were popular gifts. Carpet slippers worked in tapestry or Berlin wool 'so well calculated for birthday presents and souvenirs' were mentioned by *La Mode* in 1830, and the style of slipper shown here (unmade, but embroidered to shape; it could cost between 5s. and 7s. 6d. to turn them into slippers in the 1860s) survive in many museum collections.

THE ROUND HAT.

1. When it is all very well. 2. When it is objectionable.
3. When the Police ought to interfere.

104. Cartoon from Punch, 22 September 1855

Note: From the mid-1850s the hat reappeared to challenge the supremacy of the bonnet. *Punch* cartoons poked fun at these wide-brimmed hats which proliferated like mushrooms in the English countryside and on beaches. By 1857 the style became modified into a smaller version with dipped front brim and feather plume, worn for riding and walking and not dissimilar to the display hat in Fig. 103. The streamers which floated behind these hats were called 'follow-me-lads'.

105. Parasol, English, 1855-65

One-piece cover of printed warp-frame fabric; the colour of the centre is brown.

Note: Sangsters patented a seamless cover in 1855. Cover and lining were cut in one piece from a knitted fabric made on the warp-frame machine with a cord or fringe put around the edge to prevent stretching. Surviving examples have printed borders of flowers and motifs familiar from Paisley and other shawls, and are stretched over wire frames.

106. Shawl, English, c. 1850

Cream and black leno printed with a curving design of flowers and leaves derived from the ever-popular Indian/Paisley motifs.

Note: This shawl by Messrs Towler & Campin, Norwich is a good example of the delicate designs and precision printing for which they were well known. Competition with Paisley in Scotland led some Norwich manufacturers to lower costs by printing rather than weaving shawls. They chose to do this on carefully chosen cotton and silk surfaces like leno which had a particularly tight weave. See colour plates IX and X.

Nineteenth-century accessories

108. Stocking, English, 1851

White silk with open-work lace design.

Note: The Great Exhibition of 1851 provided an excellent showcase for British and foreign goods. This example was made and shown there by the Nottingham hosiery manufacturers I. & R. Morley. They exhibited many types of hosiery including stockings of cotton, Lisle thread and silk, and men's 'half-hose' of cotton. Many of the hosiery exhibitor's wares found their way, subsequently, into museum collections in Nottingham, Leicester, Manchester and London. The British entrants to the exhibition were commended for unequalled bleach and finish of cotton hosiery (Nottingham) and diversified range, colour and shape (Leicester).

107. Reticule, English, c. 1850

Dark-green velvet embroidered with light-green silks and with gilt-bead ornamentation and fringing. Gilt-metal chain and filigree frame with press-button catch.

Note: Women's magazines issued embroidery patterns for this type of bag which, when worked, could be sewn to a ready-made frame. Although, in the late 1820s there was a revival of tie pockets, to be superseded by attached glazed-cotton pockets integral to the skirt, the making of bags for occasional personal use or for charity bazaars did not decline. Simple shapes, complementary to fashionable dress fabrics, and decorated with embroidered cross-stitch flowers or ribbon work (1830s and 40s); painted flowers on velvet (1840s and 50s) or the perennially popular beadwork, using American Indian motifs in the 1850s, and Berlin woolwork, kept a steady flow of these articles into general use. Examples will be found in many museum collections.

109. Women's boots, c. 1850

White satin, side-laced boots.

Note: Black and white were traditional colours for women's boots and shoes, but thin fabrics, such as satin were mainly for indoor use.

110. To Brighton and Back for 3/6, Charles Rossiter, 1859

Note: Travel scenes and crowds at railway stations, race meetings, in post offices and other places of assembly were popular subject matter for Victorian genre painters. They are, of course, an invaluable source of information about the dress worn by various classes and age groups.

Hat: All but one of the men are wearing top hats of the 'stove-pipe' shape characteristic of the 1850s; the one to the right is grey. To the left the husband is trying to protect his hat with what looks like a woman's handkerchief or bonnet veil. The young man (right foreground) is wearing one of the informal styles which emerged in the late 1840s; known as a 'wide-awake' it was a soft felt hat which owed much to the round hat of the 1780s. Disputes about its origins do not detract from its popularity. Soft hats could, however, be viewed with suspicion. When the composer Franz Liszt visited New York wearing something similar in 1853 he excited police attention for wearing a 'democratic' hat. All of the women are wearing bonnets, slipping further back over the head, the necks trimmed with bavolets. The older woman (left foreground) is protecting her bonnet with a folded scarf much in the manner of a twentieth-century headscarf. The small girls are wearing modified versions of the round hat (fig. 104).

Shawls: A range of shawls and/or travelling rugs are visible. The young man's checked shawl drapes badly and is probably an inexpensive wool travelling rug. The young woman's tartan shawl looks much softer and is perhaps a winter shawl. The older woman wears a reversible shawl, the patterned lining folding back over a deeply fringed shawl folded over her lap. These could be Norwich or Paisley in origin.

Gloves: Both women in the foreground wear the plain, wrist-length gloves which were considered essential for outdoors.

Umbrellas and parasols: The older woman carries a parasol of the plainer type used in the 1840s with the cover cut in curves between the ribs. The young man holds his companion's carriage parasol. It might be made entirely of ivory, but is more likely to be white-painted wood with the small bone hook handle typical of the cheaper parasols of the decade. The large black umbrella to the back of the carriage is of the size and shape needed for wet weather.

Nineteenth-century accessories

111. Advertisement from a paper bag, c. 1860

Note: Advertisements can be a fruitful source of information especially if, as in this example, the illustrations show a wide range of the manufacturer's or shopkeeper's wares.

Hats and caps: Four types of top hat, all with slightly different brims, indicate the significance of this style; there is only one 'wide-awake'. Boys and young men wore a variety of caps after c. 1820. They were of felted wool, often with a leather peak and decorative band and sometimes a button or tassel on the crown. The straw hat (centre top) became fashionable in the mid-1840s; it was similar to those worn with sailor's uniforms at this date.

Parasols: All of the parasols have the knobbed decoration on their turned sticks and the covers with patterned decoration typical of the 1850s. Fringes were a feature but it was only after 1858 that lace parasol covers became fashionable, using black Chantilly lace (and its imitations); Bedfordshire, Maltese, Honiton, Brussels and Carrickmacross lace were also used.

112. Cartoon from Punch, 8 September 1866

Note: This cartoon pokes fun at the differing styles of clothing and headwear worn by fashionable young men in France (left) and England (right). The Englishman is wearing a type of top hat nicknamed a 'Muller-cut-down' which obviously did not impress the French.

Although for the first forty years of the century top hats were the most fashionable daytime headwear, there were variations in height, brim and shape of crown; sporting versions could be brown or grey in colour and a collapsible opera hat was patented in 1840, always known as a 'gibus'. Other styles of hat and cap which became popular can be seen in Figs. 110, 111 and 115.

ON THE BOULOGNE PIER.
(TWO ASIDES.)

Young England. "RUMMY STYLE OF 'AT!" *La Jeune France.* "DRÔLE DE CHAPEAU!"

114. Gig umbrella, 1860-1900

Black-painted wood stick with 'pine cone' handle; black cotton cover, corded at the edge; nine cane ribs with brass tips.

Note: This is an umbrella of the traditional sort which was kept in hallways to shelter visitors from the carriage to the door. These umbrellas survive in quantity as they were made over a considerable period. Dating of them can only be approximate, depending on the presence of machine stitching or the decoration on the inside cap. They could also have a green cover. In 1894 they cost between 6s. 6d. and 35s. depending upon construction.

113. Shawl, Scottish, c. 1865

Woven wool shawl in polychrome colours in cone and palmette motifs, fringed at two ends although square in construction. This is a reversible shawl from the Paisley factory in western Scotland; the technique used a double set of warp threads with weft threads not needed on either side left floating between the two.

Note: In the twentieth century, Paisley has come to mean any shawl using the cone motif and associated patterns. The Paisley factory's output was far greater than any other in Britain as it concentrated on large-scale production for a mass market. Its success lay in cheap copies of the designs of other factories, threatening Edinburgh and Norwich in succession. It was already a household name by the 1840s and was patronized by Queen Victoria. Capable of producing fine-quality results, it preferred to use the technical virtuosity of the Jacquard loom to flood the market with its wares. The reversible shawl, its great success of the 1860s, was pirated from the original work of W. H. Clabburn of Norwich who patented it in 1854 and exhibited it at the Paris exhibition in the following year.

Nineteenth-century accessories

No. 4.—AT THE DERBY.

115. Engraving from Girl of the Period, July 1869

Note: This engraving depicts a group of fashionable young women at the races, eating a picnic and surrounded by male admirers and the gypsies and entertainers who were an integral part of these occasions. This is a good-natured pastiche, suitably updated, of Frith's 'Derby Day', 1856-58 (Tate Gallery, London).

Hats: All of the young women have adopted the hairstyle of the mid-to-late 1860s, dressed high at the front and loosely braided at the back. This style required the 'Empire bonnet', worn at the front of the head and not dissimilar to the dress caps of this date with lightweight silk net, lace and ribbon decorations and loose streamers held well below the chin with a bow or flowers. The older woman (right foreground) has a respectable plain bonnet of the early 1860s and the gypsy woman wears a spotted handkerchief as a headscarf. The majority of men sport top hats (including the servant to the left) with festive tulle or silk ribbons wrapped over the hat band. The man seated on the carriage box wears a flat-crowned version of the bowler hat which Lock's produced for the Duke of Cambridge in 1865 and named

after him. The older man (right foreground) is wearing a low-crowned top hat called a 'Muller-cut-down' after a murderer identified by this headwear in 1865.

Jewellery: The young women wear pendant earrings of which there was a wide variety of styles in gold, enamel and semi-precious stones.

Shawls: The gypsy wears the warm, inexpensive tartan shawls which became associated with poorer members of society in the second half of the nineteenth century. The older woman (right) has a plain shawl, probably of good, fine wool.

Bags: The older woman (right) carries a capacious home-made bag, suitable for a day's outing.

Parasol: This is square and fringed, a style of ingenious but short-lived fashion.

116. Pair of 'pork pie' hats, 1860-65

Dark-blue velvet, trimmed with ostrich-feather tips with elastic cord to fasten under the hair.

Note: This style of hat made of dark straw or velvet with feather trimming appeared in 1859. This reappearance of the hat, admittedly in truncated form, caused great controversy amongst contemporaries; their wearers, usually youthful, were referred to as 'fast young ladies'. Perhaps this should have been the title of Augustus Egg's 'The Travelling Companions', c. 1860 (Birmingham City Art Gallery) in which two sisters are seated in a railway carriage with straw 'pork pie' hats in their laps.

117. Hats, English, 1868-70

Left, straw trimmed with pale-blue velvet and artificial flowers, with matching bow and hanging ends on an elastic cord, designed to tilt the hat over the forehead. Right, straw and cotton weave, trimmed with ruched white muslin and black velvet.

Note: These flat hats were based upon the traditional peasant head-dresses of the south of France. They were worn tilted over the forehead above the rising hairstyles of the late 1860s. As more opportunities to travel abroad came within the scope of the middle classes, fashion themes also widened beyond the traditional admiration for Paris fashions.

118. Square parasol, c. 1869

Black and white-striped silk on a folding wooden stick with a club handle. The frame has four solid metal ribs.

Note: This example is very similar to that in the *Girl of the Period* engraving (Fig. 115). The indecision about the direction in which women's fashion was going in the late 1860s stimulated fresh ideas for the parasol. Handles were thicker and many were club-shaped; covers were of odd designs. Patents were taken out for flat or slightly conical shapes and for square parasols; the last appearing in 1869. They only have four ribs and are crudely made; very much a fashion of the moment, although a few examples of these various experiments survive in museum collections.

119. Women's gloves and purse, 1860-70

Gloves of white kid stitched with brown silk and laced with a cream silk cord with tasselled ends, c. 1866. Purse of metal thread and pink silk knotted with steel beads; bead fringe and tassel and two metal sliders.

Note: Generally speaking, women's daytime gloves remained short in length until the early 1860s when gauntlet gloves became fashionable for limited use with, for example, yachting jackets. Wrist-length gloves came in a wide range of colours and there were various styles of novelty decoration in the 1850s and 1860s including ribbons, swansdown and silk fringing. The style of glove illustrated here was patented in 1866 and was made in a number of colour combinations. Evening gloves became longer in the mid-1860s and by 1871 'with the open sleeve, long kid gloves with 8 to 10 buttons have come in again'. Bead purses were still worked in quantity as gifts, for bazaars and so forth.

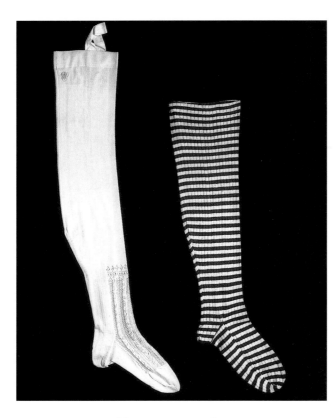

120. Women's stockings, c. 1865 and 1879

Right, white silk banded with purple, the stripes made by taking out needles at intervals, c. 1865. Left, cream silk with embroidered open-work at the front; worn by Princess Louise of Prussia when she married Arthur, Duke of Connaught, third son of Queen Victoria, in 1879.

Note: By the 1860s a number of changes were evident in the wearer's purchase and choice of stockings. Stockings (and socks) in individual wardrobes were counted in dozens rather than singly. Colours varied considerably, being sharp and bright in the early 1860s; magenta and solferino, the new aniline dyes developed from coal-tar (named after battles in the Italian War of Independence) were particularly popular. Also, with the swaying movement of the crinoline under full skirts, there were plenty of chances for stockings to be seen. The Empress Eugénie, wife of Napoleon III of France, started a trend in the early 1860s for stockings to match the dress; white became unfashionable unless the dress was white, giving way to coloured grounds ornamented with stripes, spots and embroidery in the 1860s and 1870s. Bright colours in the 1860s gave way to paler or drabber colours in the early to mid-1870s, which were then replaced by richer hues. See colour plate XIV.

121. Women's shoes, 1860-1870

Black satin with embroidery, ruched mid-blue ribbon and appliqué, layered embroidered decoration; heels covered in pale-blue silk.

Note: Women's shoes continued to be made as 'straights' despite their increasingly elaborate decoration and an increase in the height of the heel.

delaine and plain light brown taffetas. The skirt is of the striped material, with a narrow fluting of taffetas placed just inside the edge round the bottom. A short tunic of light brown taffetas is elegantly looped up with large bows of a darker shade. The edge is scalloped out, and a fringe ribbon fastened with tiny nacre buckles. The front part of the skirt is trimmed en tablier with narrow coulisse bouillonnés and flutings. The sides are trimmed with thread guipure, put on in a spiral shaped border so as to define the outline of the semi-train at the back, which is

No. 80.—PARASOLS, SUNSHADES, AND CHATELAINES.

of the darker brown shows beyond. The corsage opens to show a striped gilet fastened with nacre buttons. The sleeves have striped revers with bows of taffetas of both shades of brown, and nacre buttons.

A charming toilet for a young lady, suitable to wear at a horticultural exhibition or any summer fête, is of pale blue glacé mohair, trimmed with Pompadour bows of blue disposed into full folds, but untrimmed. A Pompadour bow is placed within each curve of the guipure trimming. The bodice is made with points, and trimmed with a small berthe trimmed to correspond with the front part of the skirt. Pompadour bows are placed upon the shoulders, and the sleeves are covered with bouillonnés and flutings in the same way as the berthe, and finished with bows to match.

122. From the Milliner, Dressmaker and Warehouseman's Gazette, July 1874

Note: The waist belts are steel-trimmed leather with steel chains for the sunshades. In 1872 *Queen* magazine suggested in answer to a query about travelling dress that a leather belt tipped with silver be worn, 'They are costly but the metal is pure and will not tarnish even with sea air, and chatelaines can be attached or separate hooks for a smelling bottle, fan or umbrella, both very useful for travelling.'

Jewellery: The chatelaine suspended from the centre belt would hook over and a sample of possible attachments is displayed. The finest examples (Fig. 126) were highly decorative items of jewellery.

Bags: A small 'chatelaine bag' is suspended from the belt (left); these could be bought with the belt or separately; usually of leather, this example has additional loops to which other small items might be attached.

Fans: The centre belt has a simple fan attached as an example of the range of accessories that could be used in this way.

Parasols and umbrellas: The central staff parasol is described as a 'Louis XV ombrelle' and is edged with feathers. This style had reappeared in 1870 and remained in fashion until 1879, echoing the styles of 100 years earlier, as did several fashions in this decade. The two examples to the left are *en-tout-cas*, one of spotted foulard, the other of brown silk. The *en-tout-cas* 'which are made large enough to serve as an umbrella as well as a parasol, are also extremely useful for travelling', came to fashionable notice in 1861 and suited the more active life which women were starting to pursue. By 1873 *Queen* magazine stated that 'En-tout-cas are now taking the place of umbrellas.' The two examples to the right are (top) a 'Marquise ombrelle' with ivory handle and cover in two colours, and a 'Trianon ombrelle' edged with striped foulard. This confusion of types and terms is typical of the 1870s.

123. Staff parasol, 1870-1880

Ivory button top with gilt metal shield and the initials 'H. G.', crown socket, rosewood stick with brass cap. The cover is of tussore silk trimmed with frills and machine lace, brown silk bow and lining.

Note: This parasol is fashionable in length, material and trimmings for the 1870s. Few of this type survive in museum collections.

124. Fashion plate from The Tailor and Cutter, 1875

Note: The gradual disappearance of the crinoline in the late 1860s, with all the fullness in skirts moved back into a bustle, had created a swathed line at the front of the garment with a longer fitted bodice. Hairstyles continued to rise above the forehead often with a looser type of chignon or braid of hair behind as a balance to the back emphasis of the bodice and skirt.

Hat: By 1874 bonnets and hats had established a new style and angle which were kept until the end of the 1880s. An oval-shaped crown with a small brim was worn at a diagonal line over the back of the head, revealing all of the curled front hair and held securely over the knot of hair on the crown of the head. This example depicts most of the fashionable elements; swathed fabric over the crown of the bonnet, plumes, groups of feathers and flowers tucked under the brim.

Jewellery: Small pendant earrings which might be of pearl or gold.

Gloves: An essential accessory with outdoor dress, these would be of plain leather.

Umbrella: This could be an *en-tout-cas* of the type *Queen* magazine suggested was replacing umbrellas in 1873. They could be covered with twilled silk or shot Venetian silk in black, blue or purple. The short, stout handle was malacca or bamboo with an ivory knob, mounted in silver-gilt with a chain to clip to the chatelaine or belt.

Bag: The chatelaine bag, of flared leather, is suspended from the waist by a chain. These seem to have become fashionable in Paris in the late 1850s and were featured in the *Englishwoman's Domestic Magazine* by 1861. Early versions were small flat bags, often shaped at the base to three tasselled points; made of velvet or silk to match an outfit they hung from the waist by a silk cord or hook and chain. They remained popular for the rest of the century but as bags became increasingly specialized in style and use, for travelling, visiting, indoor and formal dress, so did chatelaine bags. By the mid-to-late 1870s the silver chain and hook attached to a belt carried leather versions for outdoor wear, with sealskin also popular in the late 1860s and 1870s.

The Tailor and Cutter Type of Costume.   PLATE XVI.

125. Chatelaine bag, French, 1870-80

Brown leather with applied
copper plaques showing 'antique'
hunting scenes on the flap, body
of the bag and hook plate.
Scissor-shaped sliding catch with
leather strap and metal hook
plate for attachment to a belt.

Note: In the mid-1870s exotic flared
shapes were popular, reminiscent of
medieval styles. Other surviving bags
of this type also have flap fronts and
the distinctive scissor-shaped
fastening.

126. Chatelaine, c. 1875-1900

Copper alloy gilded with three colours, the five
ornamental plaques bordered with white metal
imitating silver. Possibly German.

Note: This example belongs to a large group, in private and public
collections, of pastiche eighteenth-century chatelaines. The
individual elements are repeated in different combinations to
provide a variety of designs. The chatelaine enjoyed periods of
popularity throughout the century, in 1871 the Princess of Wales
started to wear one, thereby
renewing interest in this accessory.
Numerous useful items could be
suspended from them;
pencils, scissors, button-
hooks, smelling salts; they
were more practical than
the watch and
implement-filled
necessaire of the
previous century.

Nineteenth-century accessories

MYRA'S PARIS PATTERNS AND MODELS

Head: Caps were worn only by the elderly; for evening wear fashionable women attached flowers, plumes or used decorative combs or pins in their hair.

Jewellery: Necklaces often included revivalist or 'primitive' motifs using a good deal of metalwork and fewer precious stones, although parures and demi-parures of diamonds or other stones might appear on the most formal occasions. Heavy bangles worn loosely around the wrist were popular with evening dress.

Gloves: These usually reached above the elbow and suede gloves for evening wear became fashionable again alongside the classic kid. They were banned for court wear by Queen Victoria in 1882 but were worn elsewhere despite royal disapproval.

Fan: One of the larger fans in a dramatic combination of stark black interleaved with pale decoration (see Fig. 129).

127. Fashion plate from Myra's Journal of Dress and Fashion, December 1884

Note: The continued emphasis at the back of women's skirts with an enlarged bustle structure to support the layers and swags of fabric produced an S-shape which, in fashion plates, suggests that women are about to fall forward under the weight of these fashions. However, the fashionable imagination was at its most exuberant, combining delicate and large-scale decoration and accessories in a confusingly unbalanced manner.

Stockings: Those on the left appear to have an open-work or embroidered design. They would match either the shoes or the dress.

Shoes: Probably pale satin with a high heel, the fronts decorated with flat bows and small buckles.

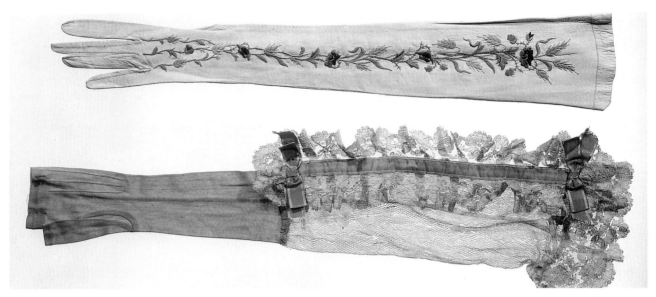

128. Woman's glove and mitten, 1875-85

Top, white kid glove embroidered with a design of flowers, leaves and wheat-ears in red, green and gold silks, possibly French. Below, mitten of grey machine-knitted silk lower arm with toning netted-lace upper arm, trimmed with grey lace and taupe ribbon, American.

Note: By the 1870s the French taste for embroidered kid gloves had influenced English and American fashions. There was a wide array of possible embroidery motifs. Dent Fownes, the English glove manufacturers, have in their collection a kidskin embroidered in polychrome silks and metal thread with different types of pointing, flower sprays, monograms, coronets and sprigs with a label 'Gloves Made to Order', allowing considerable choice to customers. As sleeves shortened for both day and evening wear and glove length increased, the use of lace, beads, ruching, printing and other techniques allowed gloves to co-ordinate with all aspects of the toilette. Mittens, always popular with older women, became fashionable again in the late 1870s, often made of expensive lace; Chantilly lace gloves cost £4 and Venetian guipure-lace gloves cost £2-3 per pair in 1879.

129. Woman's glove and fan, c. 1880-90

Glove: Light-brown kid hand and netted-silk arm with appliqué decoration, c. 1885.

Fan: Black satin leaf embroidered in gold silks and edged with gold silk lace; wooden sticks and guards painted black; black silk tassel, 1880-90.

Note: An advertisement in *Le Moniteur de la Mode* depicts similar gloves being worn with day dress in 1885. Gloves (and, more rarely, mittens) were manufactured which had a leather or fabric hand with a silk mesh or net arm, the latter embroidered or covered with appliqué to simulate lace. Dent Fownes' collection includes examples in black, ecru with bronze bead embroidery, and white with the net arms appliquéd with satin butterflies. White suede gloves were also printed above the wrist to look like black Chantilly lace. By 1897 kid evening gloves with lace arms cost as little as 6s. 10d. per pair.

130. Purses, 1839-99

Top, silver purse with finger ring, 1898/99. Centre left, shaggy bead purse of pink silk, knitted with glass and steel beads, c. 1839. Centre, leather purse with a portrait in lacquer of the Empress Eugénie, 1861-70. Centre right, mother-of-pearl purse with finger ring, 1890-99. Below centre, leather purse decorated with enamel design of flowers and swags, 1860-70. Below right, sovereign purse of embossed gilt metal, containing a spring-loaded disc to hold the coin, c. 1885-99.

Note: The continued popularity of home-made purses is demonstrated by the c. 1839 knitted pink silk and bead one. It is similar to one featured in the *Ladies' Knitting and Netting Book* in 1839. The wallet purse remained the most popular type until the 1860s. Then, from the mid-1850s, leather purses gained in popularity. Initially home-made they were superseded in the 1860s by ready-made framed purses of leather and other materials. The favourite shape was rectangular with rounded corners, a scrolled top and press-button catch, as in the lower centre two examples. By the 1870s fabric purses had virtually disappeared, replaced by leather or the same materials as fashionable handbags. The finger-ring purses were twisted around the forefinger and were used in the 1890s when the narrow line of dresses did not allow pockets. Sovereign purses were carried by men and attached by a ring to their watch chain. See colour plate VII.

131. Photograph dated 9 May 1885

Note: The importance of the development of photography as a new medium for recording individuals and groups of people is of considerable significance in the nineteenth century. However, its use for the depiction of new fashions, the manner in which they should be worn, and, by implication, the ideal physique for certain styles is a twentieth-century phenomenon. Photographs do provide a useful antidote to the idealized fashion plate. They show less extreme versions of current fashions, they indicate awkwardness of fit, and how a style might look on men and women of different stature to those depicted in magazines.

Hat: This may be a cross between a version of the 'Directoire' style which appeared between 1884 and 1886 and a straw boater. The former was a hat with a tall, rigid, tapering crown and shallow brim, often decorated with cockades and loops of ribbon. The foundation for many 1880s hats and bonnets was a coarse straw plait known as 'rustic'; it was worn throughout the year. The popularity of straw was met by an expansion in the English straw-hat industry due to technical innovations of this period. Straw boaters were increasingly popular for all outdoor activities from 1884 onwards.

Jewellery: Around her neck this woman is wearing a close-fitting metal link-chain necklace from which a diamond-shaped plaque is suspended.

Gloves: Dark, possibly suede leather.

Umbrella: This might be an *en-tout-cas* and has the looped handle typical of the 1880s.

132. Parasols, 1880-1900

Left, black satin cover, piped and trimmed with 'Spanish' lace; chip-carved ebonized wood stick with a hook at either end, 1880-85. Centre, black cotton twill cover printed with silver lines; tapering chip-carved ebonized wood handle, 1890-1910. Right, black silk twill cover opening to deepish dome, band of open-work weaving near edge, carved ebonized wood crutch handle, 1890-1900.

Note: These are examples of the plainer styles of parasol which were available in a twenty-year period which saw considerable variety in size, shape, colour and decoration. Revivals of earlier styles, the marquise, pagoda and flat parasols with numerous ribs reappeared in the 1870s, often with confusing new names. Although bright colours were mentioned in fashion magazines, few survive, except as brightly coloured linings to black satin covers. Covers were embroidered and painted with flowers and insects, and lace retained its popularity as both fabric and trimming. Some linings were printed. The commonest handles of the 1880s were of wood, often ebonized and bent by steam into curves, crooks, loops, knots, etc., although more elaborate and expensive parasols had complex carving or used lapis lazuli, porcelain or ivory for knobs. The variety was bewildering and mirrored the elaborate trimmings on all fashionable clothing in the 1880s. By the end of the 1880s, black and white moiré became fashionable for the plainer parasol foreshadowing simpler styles in the 1890s. By 1894 *Cassell's Family Magazine* reported 'sunshades favour the umbrella type, simple and plain, with slender handles of natural form in either cherrywood, bramble or thorn'. Delicate striped silks, moiré with lace insertions and chiné silks were often weighted with tin-salts and their subtle elegance can rarely be appreciated now.

133. Framed handbag, English, 1887

Fawn leather covered with red plush and embroidered in silk to commemorate Queen Victoria's golden jubilee. White metal frame and sliding catch, released by squeezing the two ends of the clasp.

Note: The small handbag evolved from the travelling bag in which necessities required on a journey could be carried separately from the main luggage. From the late 1860s there were 'muff-bags' of fur and they retained their popularity, made of plush or satin in the 1880s. Small leather bags were recommended as Christmas gifts in 1879; examples of that date were also made in sealskin to match fashionable capes and trimmings. These soft-edged bags with rounded corners were replaced, in the mid-1880s, by a hard-edged, boxy style of bag which suited the more angular, tailored fashions. Many were covered in red or blue plush to match an outfit; others were in the new range of coloured leathers as aniline dyes were adapted for dying leather.

134. Women's stockings, English, 1884

Black silk with open-work fronts and white silk embroidery. Made by B. Walton of Sutton-in-Ashfield for the trousseau of Laura Marianne Morley (née Birch) who married S. Hope Morley in 1884. The chevening was done by Miss Emma Shacklock, senior hosemender at I. & R. Morley, Fletcher Gate, Nottingham.

Note: From 1880 black stockings appeared as an alternative to the coloured stockings previously so fashionable, particularly for daywear. For most of the 1880s and 1890s shoes and stockings had to match, although in 1884 black stockings were worn with black dresses and scarlet leather shoes. By 1900 nineteen out of every twenty pairs of stockings made were black. Improvements to make the black dye fast, the dirtiness of town life and the wearing of leather footwear all combined to promote the practicality of black stockings. They could be plain, embroidered, ribbed, striped depending upon dictates of fashion. Attempts were made to revive white in the late 1880s; by 1893 Paris decreed that they were necessary for evening wear but by 1897 'one realises that their day is over except with white dresses at the seaside' (*Girl's Own Paper*, 28 August 1897). See colour plate XII.

135. The Bayswater Omnibus, George William Joy, 1895

Note: Horse-drawn omnibuses were a feature of large cities in the later years of the nineteenth century. A cross-section of society could usually be found travelling on them. From left to right, a poor woman, dressed in drab, unfashionable garments; a smart young woman; an elderly businessman, dressed for his city office; a young nurse in her distinctive uniform and a young milliner's assistant, carrying the large hat-box required to transport fashionable headwear.

Hats: The poor woman wears a simple dark bonnet tied under her chin. Wide-brimmed hats worn at an angle and trimmed with feathers were held by decorative hat-pins onto the tightly curled coiffure in the mid-1890s, and the young woman's is a typical example. The businessman wears the ubiquitous silk top hat with curled brim. The nurse wears a plain bonnet to which a veil is attached (early in the next century bonnets were so unfashionable that, in trade catalogues, they were described as 'Old Ladies' and Nurses' Bonnets'). The milliner's assistant wears a smart, wide-brimmed straw hat.

Jewellery: In the 1890s tiny brooches and pins, often of clear stones and made in the shape of crescents, stars and hearts were popular; the young woman's is in the form of a bow with a pendant pearl. Most men, by this date, wore little jewellery.

Gloves: Both the nurse and the smart young woman wear short, day-length gloves of pale suede. The businessman would also have a pair of gloves.

Parasol: Deep-pink parasol with an exceptionally long, tapering handle; the businessman is holding a tightly furled umbrella, possibly with a crook handle.

Bag: Leather metal-framed business bags could contain documents, pens and other items which their owners needed for their work. They were similar in style to travelling bags, the genesis of which can be found as early as 1826 when Pierre Godillot of Paris invented a light-framed travelling bag made of canvas. English travellers started to use something similar in the 1850s, often with woolwork embroidery (similar 'carpet' bags were taken by emigrants to America, leading to the derogatory term 'carpet-bagger'). Leather luggage also appeared in the 1850s and as it gained popularity the frames and opening and locking mechanisms improved.

Shoes: The women's shoes are plain, dark leather. The man wears boots and spats (made of box-cloth or canvas cloth in white, grey or fawn) which were worn with frock coats after 1893.

136. Woman's hat, 1892-1900

Green velvet constructed to echo the shape of a Tudor flat cap. Label of 'Liberty & Co. Artistic and Historic Costume Studio, 222 Regent Street'.

Note: Reform and artistic movements to change women's attitudes towards dress were an occasional feature of the second half of the nineteenth century. Amelia Bloomer, the American feminist, the Pre-Raphaelite circle and the Dress Reform Society used a variety of arguments and experiments to wean women away from the vagaries and discomforts of high fashion. Although the butt of *Punch* cartoons, they enjoyed some limited success in intellectual circles and, from the early 1890s until just before the First World War, Liberty's issued brochures and produced garments and accessories based upon historic and aesthetic principles. This hat or cap is quite in line with the softer wide-brimmed hats of the 1890s but without the excessive decoration usually found in this period.

137. Umbrellas, 1888-1896

Left, woman's umbrella with black silk twill cover, lock-rib frame and chased silver handle with a vinaigrette under a flap at the top, 1888. Right, man's umbrella with black silk cover, rattan cane stick and ivory handle with gilt band inscribed 'Presented to Mr I. Uridge as a mark of esteem from a few members of the Bromley Cycling Club, Oct. 1896'.

Note: By the 1870s the metal-framed umbrella was practical and ornamental, an appropriate accompaniment to the frock coat and top hat. Most improvements during the next forty years or so were aimed at making the umbrella slimmer and more compact, using, in the main, the Paragon frame. The noticeable difference in women's umbrellas, apart from size of cover, was in the ornamental nature of the handles. Semi-precious stones, silver, painted porcelain, bird's heads, carved figures, even watches were used to decorate handles and knobs.

138. Women's boots, 1890-1900

Cream kid leather with laces and decorative punching and top-stitching. Lined with pale-blue silk, the inside top edge trimmed with multi-coloured floral ribbon; the lining stamped in gold with the brand name, 'The Bective'.

Note: Sizes were standardized, in 1885 in England, in 1887 in America, and the offering of several sizes of width became more widespread. Heel heights rose to over six inches in the 1890s; shoes were more widely worn than boots. See colour plate XVII.

139. Fashion plate from Queen, 1900

Note: The fashionable silhouette for women around the turn of the century emphasized a full, rounded 'pouter-pigeon' bosom, a narrow waist and curving hips with moderate emphasis: an S with the upper curve more pronounced than the lower. It was a mature woman's physique which was particularly impressive when displayed in formal evening dress.

Head: Decorative combs, fillets and aigrettes with or without an ostrich feather were amongst the most popular ways of completing the coiffure with its soft, full, side hair and chignon placed high on the crown.

Jewellery: Many hair decorations would be described as jewellery set with the finest of diamonds or other precious stones but equally effective in paste. Tight-fitting 'chokers' or collars of pearls, diamonds or decorative beads attached to ribbon (left) had been fashionable for many years. They were particularly associated with the Princess of Wales who disguised a small scar on her neck with high collars in daytime or their jewelled equivalent in the evening. Delicate crescent and other novelty jewelled brooches retained their fashionable appeal.

Gloves: These reached high above the elbow and were probably of the Mousquetaire variety. This name denoted a style which although of a length which might warrant 20 buttons were made with only 4 to 6 buttons inside the wrist. In the late-nineteenth and twentieth centuries, button-length is the number of inches from the base of the thumb to the top of the glove rather than an actual number of real buttons.

Fans: Top right is a partly opened fan, still quite large in scale and of lace or painted gauze. The younger woman holds a feather fan which might be a fixed shape.

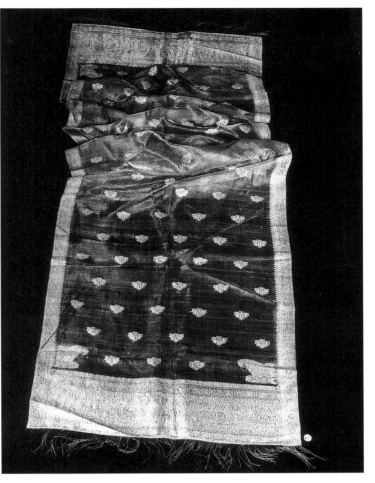

140. Shawl, c. 1900

Silver gauze with woven borders using traditional cone motifs; the central area woven with regular butterfly motifs; fringed at each end.

Note: This is an interesting example of an Indian shawl woven to western requirements. The delicate silver gauze and butterfly motifs suited English taste at this time. Although shawls are not often depicted in fashion plates of the period, the nature of evening dresses suggests that they would be essential in uncertain northern climates.

141. Fan, 1890-99

Printed silk leaf featuring photographs of seventy actors
and actresses with incised bone sticks and guards.
Known as 'Louis Felberman's Celebrity Fan'.

Note: In the last two decades of the nineteenth century and well
into the twentieth century, novelty fans were produced which
reflected popular taste in entertainment, topical issues and an
insatiable desire for novelty which is typical of this period. See
colour plates XIV and XV.

142. Spectators at Ascot Races, c. 1905

Note: The women's fashions of the early years of the twentieth century were immensely decorative using lace, embroidery, appliqué, ribbons and flowers to create an illusion of exquisite femininity. This was a stark contrast to the more business-like menswear which had an understated and uniform quality. Naturally there were exceptions and beneath the surface of sophisticated frivolity ran undercurrents of concern, both nationally and internationally, about the role of women and other disenfranchised groups in society.

Hats: Ascot was then, as it is now, a major fixture in the English summer social season. All fashionable women vied with each other to wear flattering and ultra-chic millinery. Full hairstyles, sometimes assisted by 'transformations' (false hairpieces) and a battery of long, decorative hat-pins conspired to create the illusion of hats floating upon the head rather than being worn. Curved brims, shallow crowns, quasi-tricorne shapes and toques were swathed or layered with chiffon, tulle, feathers and flowers, often with the gap between the tilt of the hat and the hair supported by a 'bandeau' covered with a 'chou' of ribbons and flowers. Colours were pale pastels; the major dark contrast being black against white. Top hats for men were black with shorter crowns than earlier.

Neckwear: All of the men in formal morning dress would have worn starched, detachable wing collars and silk cravats in discreet hues.

Jewellery: Simple pearl or gold earrings, decorative hat pins and brooches worn with the high-necked, elaborate collars of this date.

Gloves: Pastel leather or suede to the elbows to tone with the outfits of the women.

Parasols: The most elaborate is to the right of centre, it has a wavy edge and appears to be trimmed with flowers. With the exception of the one on the left which is probably a chine-printed silk, all of the others are either plain sunshades or light-coloured *en-tout-cas.*

143. Parasol, 1900-1910

Cream silk warp-frame lace embroidered by machine in chain stitch with applied braid over a silk-covered frame; painted porcelain handle with white painted stick.

Note: Lace parasols were popular in the early years of the century, as were shaded effects or bands of graduated colour and shot effects. Black and white, as with millinery, retained their popularity. Handles were often carved or opened to reveal coins or pencils. Parasols became plainer from about 1907 onwards as women's fashions generally became less extravagantly decorated.

144. Illustration from a Marshall & Snelgrove catalogue, c. 1905

Hats were an essential accessory in the early years of the century and the choice of style was considerable. This photograph of the millinery department of a major London department store indicates the luxurious surroundings within which women could select and buy hats for every type of daytime engagement.

CORPORATION STREET BIRMINGHAM
IN MARCH 1914

145. Corporation Street, Birmingham, Joseph Southall, 1914

Note: This mural of one of the major streets in one of England's largest provincial cities depicts a cross-section of local inhabitants six months before the outbreak of the First World War. Women's clothing had become much more streamlined and less exaggerated in the preceding year or so, and there is a much more recognizably modern look to their appearance.

Hats: All of the women, with the exception of the flower-seller, wear the smaller-brimmed but higher, angular, crowned hats of daytime dress. They were made of felt, velvet or coloured straw, fitted more closely to the head, with simpler trimming of contrasting ribbons and centrally placed lancer or hussar plumes which seem, uncannily, to foretell the militarism of the next four years. The flower-seller wears a plain, dark straw with flatter crown and wider brim which was available cheaply. The men's hats indicate age, occupation and status. The cart-driver has the flat wool or tweed cap which was associated with the working class but also worn by gentlemen in the country or for such sports as tennis and golf. It had gained a stiffened visor in the 1880s and the front crown fastening down to the visor had appeared in the 1890s. The young man wears a felt hat which has elements of the Homburg hat (popularized by Edward VII from the 1870s onwards) and the Trilby, a

soft-brimmed felt named after the character in du Maurier's play (1895 onwards). Both types and bowler hats could be worn in town with a lounge suit, but the frock and morning coats required a silk top hat, worn here by the older man.

Jewellery: The fashionable women wear discreet pendant earrings, possibly of gold or pearl; the woman in the centre foreground has a small cameo brooch pinned to the neckline of her blouse.

Shawls and scarves: Two of the women wear fur stoles, the most distinctive being that with the accompanying muff. The markings on the latter are not those of an animal and this may be an example of fox fur dyed, or bleached, to create the design. Furs had been prominently displayed at the Exposition Universelle in Paris in 1900 and sable, ermine, mink, skunk, marten and others were readily available. Stoles added a luxurious and sinuous accessory to the simpler, narrower lines of clothing.

Gloves: Plain wrist-length suede or leather gloves were worn in the daytime by both men and women.

Bag: The woman on the far right carries a neat leather handbag. Most bag leathers were dyed in Germany where the vast chemical industry could produce an impressive range of colours. Germany was also a major centre for metal bag frames and fittings.

Stockings: The woman with the dog wears stockings to tone with her skirt and shoes.

Shoes and boots: Two of the fashionable women are wearing high-heeled Balmoral boots, the legs of a paler colour, contrasting with the patent golosh. One pair are laced (right) the other buttoned. By 1900, confusingly, the name had been shortened to 'bal'. The woman in the centre wears laced shoes with wide ribbon laces. The flower-seller's black laced boots are so sturdy that they might be a man's pair (see the young man's pair for comparison). The older man wears laced Oxford shoes.

146. Woman's hat, c. 1912

Woven from shaded chenille thread with a wide, shallow crown and narrow, curved brim. The front is decorated with the head and wings of an owl.

147. Motor sunshade, 1910-20

Cream plastic and ebonized wood handle, marquise hinge at the top; silk cover, solid metal frame labelled 'S. Fox & Co. Ltd Arcus'.

Note: The gradual introduction of the motor car in the last years of the nineteenth century and the early years of the twentieth stimulated manufacturers to produce the appropriate parasol to protect the face from wind and dust. Not dissimilar to the earlier carriage parasol, the major difference was that handles were larger and that versions were made which could fold up into a leather case 'to hang on the arm or in the car'. Larger motor shades, such as this one, can be recognized by the presence of the marquise hinge. They were made into the 1920s but became rarer as cars were enclosed and speeds increased.

148. Woman's opera bag, French, c. 1910

Box-shaped flapped bag of beige leather, lined with silk, and fitted with twist knob purse, mirror, ivory writing tablet and gold pencil, opera glasses, folding fan and swansdown powder-puff. Long beige silk carrying cord with tassels.

Note: The diversity of styles of bag and their cost was increasing throughout the early years of the century. This specialist evening bag is an example of the ingenuity of the manufacturer in being able to meet the needs of affluent customers.

149. 'Smart Boas for Spring Wear', advertisement by Messrs. Swan & Edgar Ltd., 1916

The text accompanying the illustration reads as follows, '1. Marabout and Ostrich feather collar . . . 8/6. 2. Ostrich Feather Ruffle with Satin Bow . . . 12/9. 3. Ostrich and Marabout Feather Cravat . . . 17/9. 4. Marabout and Ostrich Collar, finished Oxidised or Gilt Button . . . 25/6. 5. Flat Ostrich Feather Ruffle, made of two strands, finished Satin and Feather Rosette . . . 18/9. 6. Full Ostrich Feather Ruffle . . . 31/6.'

Note: Boas and furs enjoyed enormous popularity from about 1914 onwards. The anti-plumage lobby did not object to the use of ostrich feathers. These could be plucked from the tail feathers of a live bird without harming it, and ostriches were farmed in South Africa, North America and the south of France to supply the millinery and stole manufacturers. The various styles of hat are the high-crowned 'postilion' style (3), the wide-brimmed but acute angled variants of the three-cornered hat (2, 4 and 6), the newly fashionable Spanish style, simply trimmed (5) and a close-fitting rounded toque (1) which seems to foretell the 1920s' cloche. The plainer lines of clothing were softened by these lively and luxurious accessories.

150. Woman's stocking, 1910-20

Black cotton with elaborate decoration, probably woven on a Jacquard loom.

Note: In the late 1880s and 1890s there were a number of patents adapting the Jacquard to various knitting machines which enabled open-work stockings to be made relatively cheaply. The most expensive, however, had insertions of handmade lace and by July 1914, Paris houses had complex insertions, such as swallows or curving snakes alongside the traditional diamond-shaped ones. The narrower skirts which revealed the ankles and part of the leg, and the fashion for energetic dances such as the tango, showed off such stockings to perfection.

151. Woman's hat, French, 1914

Glossy, tightly woven claret-coloured Bangkok straw trimmed with a toning ostrich feather and gathered black velvet ribbon. Label of 'Lambert Bernheim, Paris'.

Note: Paris was unoccupied during the First World War and it became a major entertainment centre for soldiers on leave. Its couturiers and milliners produced lively feminine fashions which seemed, intentionally, to ignore the horrors of the growing conflict.

152. Dorothy bag, 1919

Black silk satin with pointed 'capes'. Embroidered with metal beads, some of which are tinted pink or green. Silk drawstring slotted through crochet-covered rings. Pink silk lining.

Note: Dorothy bags were soft fabric alternatives to the leather bags of the latter years of the nineteenth century. They were well-suited to the slimmer lines of women's clothing from about 1907 onwards and were both professionally and home-made. The advent of war gave an added boost to their popularity as the Germans had become the leading producers and exporters of top-quality leather bags, and the supply ended with the commencement of hostilities in 1914. Fabric remained popular for some years after the war, and this example would have been a stylish accompaniment to a dress with tasselled points.

153. Woman's hat, ?English, c. 1924

Sports hat with the crown made of alternate segments of white suede and suede printed with multi-coloured Paisley-style patterns. Scarf of patterned silk with a deep fringe at each end.

Note: Leather hats in this variant of the cloche style were popular for motoring; printed suede was also used for women's shoes at this time. The cloche hat was *the* hat of the 1920s, usually made of soft felt with minimal decoration. The brim was gradually pared away almost completely. The streamlined image was a conscious one - in 1923 Aldous Huxley described his heroine in *Antic Hay* as wearing 'a small sleek black hat that looked as if it were made of metal'.

154. Woman's bag, French, c. 1924

Framed handbag of black and gold leather and green felt with applied Egyptian-style bird motifs in gold and black. A gold braid handle and lining of ruched yellow satin with two pockets, each lined with lime-green satin. Matching covered mirror.

Note: Although Egyptian motifs became especially fashionable after the discovery of Tutankhamun's tomb in 1922, there had been interest in Europe in exotic goods, whether Far or Near Eastern, for a number of years.

155. 'Fashions at Ascot', press photograph, June 1927

Note: Racing at Ascot was an integral part of the English social season but, for many, it was as much a fashion parade as a sporting event. As was usual at this date and, to a limited extent throughout the century, there was a uniform style of menswear on formal occasions. This recalls the *Hatters' Gazette* comment of 1903 that 'the frock coat and tall hat are absolutely essential as a foil to the elegantly gowned woman.'

Hats: The man in the foreground is wearing a light-grey top hat with a silk band; behind the car a black top hat can be seen. Male racegoers in the background wear soft caps with peaks with three-piece suits. Both women wear picture hats, made from fibre straws such as baku or sisal decorated with flowers or ribbons. These had brims which were wider at either side of the face and narrower at the neck.

Jewellery: Both women wear the fashionable elongated double row of beads of the late 1920s. Pearls or glass beads were equally popular.

Gloves: The man's gloves, probably of suede, are tucked under his arm. They would be wrist-length with one button; the women wear pale kid.

Bags: The older woman carries a dark bag decorated with paler motifs; it is probably of fabric attached to a metal frame. Behind this is a soft leather container, possibly to hold binoculars and umbrellas. The younger woman holds a Dorothy bag with a design which suggests a Paisley style of appliqué or embroidery.

Umbrella: The older woman holds a fashionable short, stubby umbrella with unfurled cover. See colour plate XVI.

Stockings: Both women wear light-coloured stockings, probably silk, although by this date there were many ranges of artificial silk (rayon) types. Flesh tones, grey and, from 1926 'various shades of sunburn [sic] stockings', were characteristic of the late 1920s.

Shoes: For women, single-bar shoes, fastened with a button and with a Louis heel of at least 1½ inches in height were popular and available in a wide range of colours. Fewer styles of boot and many more styles of shoe were worn by men. The use of spats by the men in formal dress indicates a traditional compromise: shoes might be worn but there would be no sign of a sock.

156. Shawl, ?English, c. 1925-30

Black silk crepe machine-embroidered with a pattern of stylized roses in vivid pink, orange, magenta, blue and brown; the lining is of orange velvet; the shawl is 52 inches square.

Note: A vibrant example of Art Deco style, this shawl would have both enlivened and softened the narrow lines of women's clothes in the late 1920s.

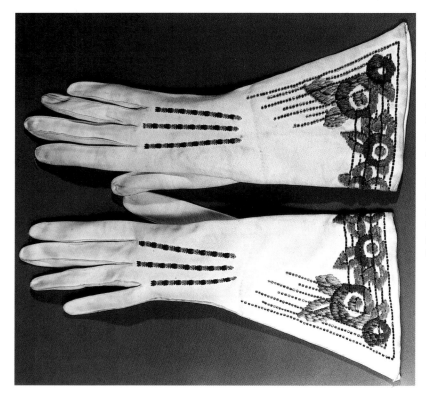

157. Women's gloves, French, c. 1925-30

Beige suede with three embroidered points in red, grey and gold thread on the back of the hand. The gauntlets are embroidered with Art Deco-stylized flowers worked in pink and grey chenille and silver glass beads. Made by Alexandrine, Paris.

Note: Although the simpler lines of women's clothing in the postwar period reinforced a movement towards much plainer gloves, there was still a wide range of materials and colours available. The gauntlet glove was particularly fashionable in the 1920s and 1930s.

159. Women's bags, c. 1925-38

Left, an evening bag of black mesh tambour beaded with yellow, red, black and purple glass beads in an Art Deco style (see also Figs. 156-8). Frame of imitation ivory, c. 1925-30. Top right, a daytime pochette of green rexine with chromium frame and twist-knob fastening, c. 1930-35. Below right, a flapped evening bag of shell-pink rayon satin with a monogram of yellow bakelite plastic; used on a cruise in 1938.

158. Parasol, ?English, c. 1921

Crêpe de Chine cover printed with pink roses and grey-green grapes; the weight of the fabric could indicate that a dress material was used to co-ordinate an ensemble. The long handle is cane.

Note: This almost geometric arrangement of flowers and fruit presages the Art Deco style which became popular after the Exposition des Arts Decoratifs in Paris in 1925. However, the innovation of the post-1919 period was that of short, stubby parasols. In 1924 the *Tatler* reported 'As the hats increase in size the sunshades become ridiculously smaller.' The lavish and often witty decoration of Art Deco ensured the continuation of its popularity throughout the 1920s and early 1930s (see Figs 156 and 157).

Note: It was only in the 1920s that a handbag became an integral part of a woman's outfit. As standards of design and production improved to combat the growth in imports there was a move towards co-ordinating fashion accessories. In 1930 the British Colour Council was set up with the specific aim of standardising colour in British industry. Soon seasonal shade cards were being issued and by the mid-to-late 1930s it was possible to find matching fabrics, gloves, shoes and handbags in the latest colours. By 1938 *Vogue's* 'Shophound' commented that 'matched up accessories are a short cut to chic'.

160. Illustration from a Marshall & Snelgrove catalogue, 1929

Shawls were worn to considerable effect over the narrow dresses of the 1920s although, even at sale prices, they were expensive luxuries: many of them were made of the finest silk or cashmere and imported from Europe and the Far East. Deep fringes were popular and the shawl could be arranged to mirror the asymmetrical hemlines of the late 1920s.

161. Fashion plate from Le Tailleur Practique, 1929

Note: By the late 1920s many designers and magazines were anticipating the longer skirts and more feminine lines of the 1930s. This fashion plate suggests something of the crisp tailoring which characterized the 1930s but the accessories are archetypally 1920s.

Hats: The sleek style of the cloche with its almost metallic helmet appearance can be seen on the head of the woman to the right. Trimmings were often confined to one side of the head, as in this example. The woman to the left wears a style suggestive of the work of couture milliners such as Caroline Reboux: the felt at the sides of the basic shape is folded into intricate pleats or ridges and held by stitching. It had an improvized quality which contrasted with the uncompromising helmet cloche.

Gloves: Both women wear plain, light-coloured gloves, probably of leather. The only decoration is the stitching on the back of the hand.

Bags: The woman to the right carries a flapped pochette or 'underarm bag'. Although the woman on the left has a traditional style of framed bag with a short strap, she holds it like a pochette. This new variant of the handbag, a Dorothy bag or large purse carried in the hand was first noted in 1916. By 1920 it had acquired a vertical wrist or thumb loop on the back, and by the mid-1920s it was a flapped rectangular bag whose uncluttered lines matched the narrow silhouette which was so fashionable.

Stockings: Both women wear plain, pale-coloured hosiery of silk or rayon.

Shoes: Two classic shapes of the 1920s, both with high Louis heels, are depicted. To the left a two-tone bar strap shoe, to the right a dark court shoe with pale trimming.

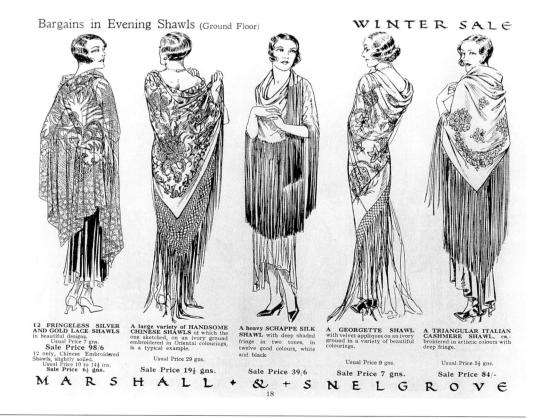

Bargains in Evening Shawls (Ground Floor)   WINTER SALE

12 FRINGELESS SILVER AND GOLD LACE SHAWLS in beautiful designs.
Usual Price 7 gns.
Sale Price 98/6
12 only, Chinese Embroidered Shawls, slightly soiled.
Usual Price 10 to 14½ ins.
Sale Price 6½ gns.

A large variety of HANDSOME CHINESE SHAWLS of which the one sketched, on an ivory ground embroidered in Oriental colourings, is a typical example.
Usual Price 29 gns.
Sale Price 19½ gns.

A heavy SCHAPPE SILK SHAWL with deep shaded fringe in two tones, in twelve good colours, white and black.
Sale Price 39/6

A GEORGETTE SHAWL with velvet appliques on an ivory ground in a variety of beautiful colourings.
Usual Price 9 gns.
Sale Price 7 gns.

A TRIANGULAR ITALIAN CASHMERE SHAWL, em-broidered in artistic colours with deep fringe.
Usual Price 5½ gns.
Sale Price 84/-

MARSHALL + & + SNELGROVE
18

117   118

**162. Charcoal drawing, George Belcher,
1925-1930**

The idealized nature of shopping promoted in
advertisements (Figs. 160 and 161) is challenged in this
humorous drawing. The large customer has adopted
fashionable accessories - a cloche hat, neat handbag and
strap shoes - but is perhaps less able to find narrow
dresses in her size.

83   "Imperial London" 1935

163. Imperial London, print, 1935

The contrast between the traditionally dressed older
man in his city 'uniform' of top hat, cravat, morning
coat, pin-striped trousers, shoes with spats, carrying a
tightly furled umbrella and wearing gloves, and the
young men, is emphatic. It is attitudinal as well as
generational, for the young men herald a more informal
relaxed future. They enjoy the sleek modern lines of a
powerful sports car and they dress, even in town, as for
an outing in the country, The bold checks of cap and
suit and casual striped scarf suggest a wish for comfort
and a disregard of formal styles of dress.

SIMPSON 202 PICCADILLY, REGENT 2002

164. Advertisement for Men's Hats, Simpson's of Piccadilly, 1938

Note: Lighter felts and different methods of construction for hats were used by manufacturers who were keen to ensure that men did not stop wearing hats because of their formality and restrictive nature. The two major successes of the early to mid-century, the boater and the snap-brim felt (Trilby hat) were essentially lightweight and informal hats. The growing emphasis on sports and leisure wear is a feature of advertisements in the 1930s.

165. Man's hat, late 1930s

Black felt Homburg hat with the label of James Howell & Co. Ltd., Cardiff. Worn by a clergyman in the late 1930s.

Note: The Foreign Secretary Anthony Eden was responsible for the fashionable revival of a tall-crowned black version of the Homburg hat. Except for the most formal occasions which required bowlers or top hats, the perennially fashionable hat for men in the 1920s and 1930s was not the Homburg but the snap-brim felt. It was much worn by gangsters in American films of the 1930s but this did not diminish its popularity.

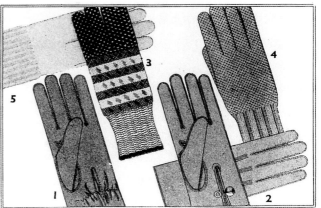

166. 'Rego for Style', advertisement, 1936

Note: The descriptive nature of this advertisement for Rego Clothiers Ltd's hats and gloves needs little explanation apart from drawing attention to the formal hierarchy of men's hats: bowler at the top of the list, then soft felt hats and finally caps. Sports hats, not illustrated, would be similar to those in Fig. 164, although the man who bought from Rego rather than at Simpson's paid less than half the latter's prices.

167. 'Jaeger for Men', advertisement, c. 1934

Note: By the 1930s men's gloves had evolved into the classic styles and were made of materials – leather or wool – which could still be purchased over fifty years later. The growing importance of casual and sportswear is reflected in the range of hats, gloves and shoes produced for these occasions.

168. Woman's pochette, 1937

Black suede with applied 'features' in black and red patent. Zip-fastening top. A typical example of the designs popularized by the Surrealist school of art in the late 1930s. The most famous exponent of translating this style to dress and accessories was Elsa Schiaparelli, the Italian couturier who worked in Paris. After the first Surrealist exhibition in Britain in 1936, a wide range of unusual accessories became available. This example was bought at Marshall & Snelgrove's department store in 1937.

Note: The zip fastener was introduced into Britain in 1919 and used on handbags from the mid-1920s. It was not used on dresses until the mid-1930s.

169. 'New Hats for Autumn & Winter', trade catalogue advertisement, 1939

Top, a black felt Florentine-style hat and spotted veil with a hat pin in the form of a parrot. Bottom, an Austrian-style sports hat in mustard-coloured felt.

Note: Both examples are high-crowned hats of the type which became popular in the second half of the 1930s. From around 1934 onwards milliners began to experiment with two devices not used for over a decade: height of crown and width of brim. A Tyrolean style was introduced as a reflection of a fascination with Austria; this also inspired the dirndl (skirt) and peasant blouse. The 'Florentine' hat became fashionable in the mid-1930s; its tall crown tapered at the top and leant forwards over a low, upwardly curving brim; it remained popular throughout the late 1930s. By 1936 there were many varieties of hat including ones influenced by Surrealist art. Schiaparelli designed a shoe hat in 1935, a lamb cutlet hat, a basket of fruit and so forth. 'The madder the hat, the smarter it is' was *Vogue's* view in 1935.

Twentieth-century accessories

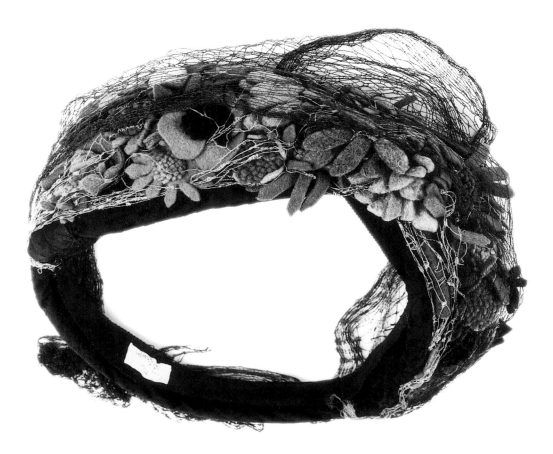

170. Woman's hat, c. 1945

Velvet base covered with appliqué felt flowers in bright colours and trimmed with a net; made in the bandeau style.

Note: During clothes rationing between 1941 and 1948 a great deal of ingenuity was required to produce attractive clothing and accessories. Hats were not rationed but considerable re-use of materials or use of non-traditional materials was found. Scarves were often substituted for hats (Fig. 171).

171. Advertisement for Mayfair scarves, September 1944

No. 39: 'Zeena. Plain fine wool Scarf. Two scarves make an attractive set – one for head turban and the second for neck . . . 4/10.' No. 40: 'Welbeck. Brushed mohair scarves. Beautifully soft and warm . . . 54/-.' No. 41: 'Eskdale. Smart check design makes this very soft woven Angora and wool scarf very attractive . . . 10/11.' No. 42 'Suzy. A becoming turban in soft rayon yarn, very easy to wear . . . 7/3.' No. 43 'Sandra. Soft woven pure Shetland makes this cosy and well-fitting Hood just right for the cooler days . . . 14/6.' No. 44 'Diane. Shilling spot fine wool square, so soft and light. Ideal for head wear (as sketch). Plain ground with contrasting spot . . . 22/11.'

Note: Neither scarves nor hats were rationed in the Second World War (1939-45) but the female civilian population, subject to air-raids and a multiplicity of problems whether at work or at home, preferred going hatless or wore turbans, hoods, headscarves (as here) or knitted caps. The crocheted snood, introduced by Schiaparelli in 1935 was also used to keep the hair tidy. The adaptability of scarves, as invention overtook necessity, assured their continued place in women's wardrobes. A square or rectangle of wool, cotton or rayon (later of silk, artificially-made fibres and mixtures) which can keep the neck and shoulders warm, the hair tidy, and adds colour and individuality inexpensively was, and is, an invaluable accessory.

Twentieth-century accessories

172. Woman's scarf, English, 1945

Moygashel printed with a multi-coloured design; bought at Bourne & Hollingsworth in 1945.

Note: The optimistic slogans and messages mirror the view that after the war ended all sorts of goods and services would, miraculously, return to normal again.

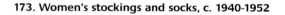

173. Women's stockings and socks, c. 1940-1952

Left, brown Lisle, the toe and heel have been cut off and reseamed under the foot; an ex-ATS stocking bought for 2s. 6d., c. 1940-45. Centre, hand-knitted mercerized cotton with wool top, heel and toe, 1941. Right, chocolate-coloured Lisle, circular knit with mock fashioning marks; label 'St. Margaret, Regd.' and a Utility mark. Made by Corah Ltd., Leicester, 1942-52. Below, socks of fawn wool with Utility mark, 1942-52.

Note: A clothing ration book of 1947/8 is also shown; as one of the last it is mostly complete. In 1941 stockings required two coupons and when available were of heavier weights to last longer. Ex-ATS stockings, like those illustrated were available in Midlands towns without coupons. Many women wore ankle socks, stained their legs or knitted their own as the hosiery industry used its reduced workforce to produce the men's socks and stockings needed for the war effort. The Utility Scheme, established by the Civilian Clothing Act in 1941, set standards for the manufacture of clothes and remained in force until 1952.

174. Women's footwear, 1942-1948

Brown suede, top-stitched in white, with ridged crepe soles. The label on the insole is 'Magic Moccasins' and there is a CC41 (Utility) mark.

Note: Sturdy and sensible footwear was not wholly a wartime necessity, similar styles had become available in the 1930s as interests in outdoor pursuits increased. When the rationing of goods was introduced in 1941, five coupons were needed for a new pair of women's shoes. Under the Limitation of Supplies Order of September 1941, footwear firms were required to produce 50 per cent of their shoes to the Utility standard.

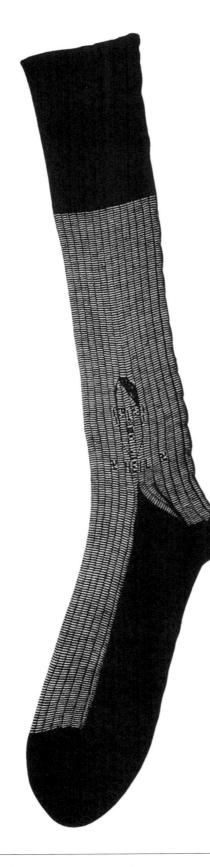

175. Men's sock, c. 1939-45

Black and white wool sock with Hitler's face, 'Heil' and two swastikas at the ankle. Made by Allen, Solly & Co. Ltd.

Note: Making light of wartime and the enemy found its expression in many ways. For less frivolous buyers there was also a Churchill sock. The majority of men in civilian life wore plain, argyle-patterned or hand-knitted woollen socks; in essence whatever they could get hold of, just like their female counterparts.

176. Women's hats, c. 1945-1953

Left, mandarin-style hat in black felt, made by Aage Thaarup, mid-1940s. Centre, dark-grey felt by Christian Dior, early 1950s. Right, black/pink shot velvet with black and pink osprey feathers. Made by Madame Vernier, early 1950s.

Note: This collection of hats was worn by the great ballerina Dame Margot Fonteyn. She, like many other elegant women in the immediate postwar period was influenced by the 'New Look' launched by Christian Dior in 1947. The enthusiastic reception of this formal, extravagant style with narrow-waisted, full-skirted dresses in a much longer length and enhanced by co-ordinated accessories reflected women's desire for a more luxurious and feminine style after the utilitarian severity of wartime. Hats were either large and decorated, or small, chic pill-boxes, boaters and 'bonnets' worn on the back of the head.

177. Woman's umbrella, 1948

'New Look' umbrella, bought in Paris. Wooden twisted, square-section hook handle with a red, white and blue-checked rayon cover over ten ribs. With matching case, bone ferrule and open cap.

Note: During the war many firms practically ceased umbrella production, making goods for the war effort instead. Between 1942 and 1947 umbrellas could only be made under licence.

Twentieth-century accessories

178. Women's stockings, c. 1945

Taupe cotton with a CC41 mark on the foot.

Note: Cotton was a long-lasting fabric for stockings but, during wartime and immediately afterwards, the great luxury was nylon stockings, only available from American sources, usually by contacts with GIs and their families and friends.

179. Women's shoes, 1945-48

Brown suede and leather with a daisy decoration applied to the front of the shoe and platform soles.

180. Women's sandals, c. 1947-1950

Red suede with peep toes, cut-out decoration and crossover straps over the arch of the foot and a strap around the heel. Label of Dolcis.

Note: This is a typical style of footwear associated with the 'New Look' introduced by Christian Dior in the late 1940s.

for Ascot
A wonderful picture hat in pink crinoline, with curled ostrich feathers.
also available in navy, black or white.   £9 . 9 . 0
Soft pouchy bag in grosgrain, navy or black. size 10 x 6 with 4½ in. base.
                                                            £6 . 19 . 6
Fine French suède elbow-length gloves in navy, brown, pastel pink,
grey, beige or black.   £3 . 15 . 6
Elegant platform shoes in grosgrain. Navy, brown or black.
American sizes 5—8½.   £5 . 9 . 6

Note: These styles are typical of the type of accessories worn with the 'New Look' in the late 1940s and early 1950s. Navy and black became classic colours for shoes and bags and remain so up to the present day.

Hat: An example of the wide picture hat decorated with feathers or a veil which drew upon Edwardian fashions for inspiration.

Jewellery: Pearl or gold earrings and pearl necklaces of one, two or three strands were worn by women of all social classes. Good imitation pearls were relatively inexpensive and often given as gifts to young women.

Gloves: Elbow-length gloves were often worn on formal occasions in the 1950s and were made in suede and kid leathers.

Bag: Professionally manufactured bags, top-fastening with steel or lacquered brass frames, replaced wartime shoulder bags or home-made pochettes. A 'good handbag' was usually chosen for its ability to match shoes, dress or suit rather than for its individuality.

Shoe: Although Dior had shown 'pointed Spanish pumps' with the New Look they were not fashionable in Britain until later in the 1950s. Square-toed shoes (with or without peep-toes) on a platform sole and high heel were very popular.

182. Women's hats, c. 1948-58

Left, black velvet and fur felt by Renée Pavy, Mayfair, 1957-58. Top centre, grey feathers over pink silk tulle, with label 'Charles Batten for Renée Pavy', c. 1948-50. Bottom centre, brown velvet covered with iridescent sequins, with label 'Erik de Paris', 1952-54.

Note: This group of hats was worn by Mrs Hill of Denton Park, Yorkshire. They demonstrate the fashion for small, close-fitting, brimless bonnets, generally worn on the back of the head and revealing the forehead.

Twentieth-century accessories

183. Women's handbags, 1950-1970

Back left, bucket-type bag in brown plastic (depth 29 cm), c. 1950-60. Back right, afternoon bag in chocolate-brown grosgrain with covered brass frame, c. 1950-1955. Front left, day bag of white painted metal plaques with white plastic frame and chain; lining of black taffeta, c. 1965-1970. Front right, evening bag of lacquered brass covered with black ribbed silk; the front lets down to reveal a gathered pocket and large fitted mirror, 1950.

Note: This group of bags provides a brief history of the possible range of style and use over two decades. The stiffened 'bucket' shape introduced from France was the ideal size for young women who worked. An open top meant that it was exempt from purchase tax. The afternoon and evening bags demonstrate the continuing demand for different sizes and styles of bag to complement more formal occasions. The white bag epitomises the youthful enthusiasm for novelties in the late 1960s, and pays homage to Paco Rabanne's futuristic dresses made from plastic discs.

184. Woman's handbag, c. 1955

Clear plastic decorated with pink plastic shells. Handle and frame of stiffened white kid. Bought in America from Saks of Fifth Avenue, New York and used by the ballerina Dame Alicia Markova.

Note: In 1948 the government imposed a purchase tax of 100 per cent on leather goods. Although this was lowered in 1952 it gave added impetus to the production of a synthetic substitute for leather. Vynide, a fabric coated with polyvinyl chloride, was hard-wearing, lightweight, washable and could be impressed to simulate texture. In 1948 Woollands offered a white Vynide bag imitating morocco leather for £2 5s. 1d. By the following year *Vogue* was stating 'Plastic bags have improved beyond recognition, so better a good plastic than a poor leather.' The Americans had led the way in developing and using plastics during and after the Second World War and this bag is an example of their inventive and witty approach to its application.

Postscript

The past fifty years have seen a great many changes in design, materials, techniques and the demands of the wearers of fashionable accessories. This short section offers a glimpse of some of the apparently limitless possibilities. As previously, the emphasis is on female requirements and what are now called unisex accessories.

Modern classics and seasonal variations: Chanel

Perhaps one of the most signficant figures of twentieth century fashion design is Coco Chanel. Alongside her considerable skill in designing clothes which flattered women and were comfortable to wear, she believed that accessories and scent (Chanel No 5 was launched in the 1920s) were an essential ingredient in the complete look. The House of Chanel is forever associated with two-tone court shoes in beige and black, which she first wore in the 1920s; costume jewellery, which includes large imitation pearls and gilt chains, and handbags – the much copied quilted leather shoulder bag with its characteristic long chain and leather strap (185) and the more formal top stitched bag with a short strap (187). Even espadrilles, the simplest of beach shoes, could become chic in a two tone combination of black and white (186). Chanel's use of interlinking initials as a discreet logo has been much emulated by other leading designers and makers.

185

186

187

188

Modern classics and seasonal variations: millinery and Rolex

Hat making is a seasonal art and it has always attracted talented and ingenious makers. This example of stripped coq feathers was designed by leading milliner Philip Treacy for a *Harper's Bazaar* photo shoot in 1993. It is witty but also demonstrates an ingenious use of materials.

The Rolex watch has, in contrast, retained many of the features which established it as a modern classic earlier in the century. These distinctive watches, made for men and women, have a timeless elegance.

189

190

191

Modern classics and seasonal variations: tights and socks

Tights, stockings and socks are now part of the overall seasonal
look, though one development of recent years is the classic status
accorded to opaque stockings and tights. Major chain stores, such
as Marks and Spencer, sell thousands of opaque and semi-opaque
tights such as those seen in the Lycra promotion on the previous
spread (190). Here they are accompanied by Patrick Cox's high-
heeled shoes; the excessive heel height is a late 1990s fashion
statement. International companies such as Wolford choose
colours and designs such as Amira to complement or contrast
with a new season's gaments (191). Specialist retailers, like the
Sock Shop, have even added wit to the humble sock (192).

193

Modern classics and seasonal variations: alternative footwear

From the late 1960s, Birkenstocks have offered a natural form of footwear for both men and women. The heel cup and 'footbed' follow and support the natural contous of the foot. Many styles ar made but the original two strapp 'Arizona' is a perennial bestseller.

Trainers or running shoes such as these produced by Puma have become another unisex classic and are worn by all age groups. They cushion the foot and offer a sense of purposeful fitness even to wearers who loath real exercise.

194

Bibliography

Adburgham, A., *Shops and Shopping 1800-1914*, Allen & Unwin, 1981

Alexander, D., *Retailing in England During the Industrial Revolution*, Athlone Press, 1970

Alexander, H., *Fans*, Batsford, 1984

Amphlett, H., *Hats: A History of Fashion in Headwear*, Richard Sadler, 1974

Anon., *Glove Story*, Dents, n.d.

Anon., *A Short History of ... the Glovers Company*, London, 1950

Armstrong, N., *A Collector's History of Fans*, Studio Vista, London & New York, 1974

Armstrong N., *The Book of Fans*, Colour Library International, 1978

Baines, B., *Fashion Revivals*, Batsford, 1981

Beck, S.W., *Gloves, Their Annals and Associations*, London, 1883

Becker, V., *Antique and Twentieth-Century Jewellery: A Guide for Collectors*, NAG Press Ltd, 1980

Blum, S.(ed.) Victorian Fashions and Costumes from Harper's Bazaar 1867-1898, Dover, New York, 1974

Blum, S.(ed.), *Ackermann`s Costume Plates: Women's Fashions in England 1818-1828*, Dover, New York, 1978

Bradfield, N., *Costume in Detail*, Harrap, 1968

Bradford, E., *Four Centuries of European Jewellery*, Spring Booksellers, 1953

Buck, A., *Dress in Eighteenth Century England*, Batsford, 1979

Buck, A., *Victorian Costume and Costume Accessories*, Ruth Bean, 1984

Byrde, P., *The Male Image: Men's Fashions in Britain 1300-1970*, Batsford, 1979

Byrde, P., *A Visual History of Costume: The Twentieth Century*, Batsford, 1986

Clabburn, P., *The Norwich Shawl*, HMSO, 1995

Clark, F., *Challenge to Fashion, Gloves 1600-1979*, Worthing Museum, 1979

Clark, F., *Hats*, Batsford, 1982

Cody Collins, C., *Love of a Glove*, New York, 1947

de Courtais, G., *Women's Head-dress and Hairstyles*, Batsford, 1973

Cumming, V., *Gloves*, Batsford, 1982

Cumming, V., *A Visual History of Costume: The Seventeenth Century*, Batsford, 1984

Cunnington, C.W., *English Women's Clothing in the Nineteenth Century*, Faber, 1937

Cunnington, C.W., *English Women's Clothing in the Present Century*, Faber, 1952

Cunnington, C.W. & P. and Beard, C., *A Dictionary of English Costume 900-1900*, A & C Black, 1960

Cunnington, C.W. & P., *Handbook of English Costume in the Seventeenth Century*, Faber, 1972

Cunnington, C.W. & P., *Handbook of English Costume in the Eighteenth Century*, Faber, 1972

Cunnington, C.W. & P., *Handbook of English Costume in the Nineteenth Century*, Faber, 1970

Dorner, J., *Fashion in the Twenties and Thirties*, Ian Allen, 1973

Dorner, J., *Fashion in the Forties and Fifties*, Ian Allen, 1975

Earnshaw, P., *A Dictionary of Lace*, Shire Publications, 1982

Eley, A.W., *Stockings*, Hosiery Trade Journal Ltd, 1953

English, W., *The Textile Industry*, Longmans, 1969

Ewing, E., *Fur in Dress*, Batsford, 1981

Ewing, E., *A History of Twentieth Century Fashion*, Batsford, 1986

Evans, J., *A History of Jewellery 1100-1870*, Faber, 1970

Farrell, J., *Umbrellas and Parasols*, Batsford, 1986

Farrell, J., *Socks and Stockings*, Batsford 1992

Flower, M., *Victorian Jewellery*, Cassell, 1967

Foster, V., *Bags and Purses*, Batsford, 1982

Foster, V., 'A Garden of Flowers', *Costume* 14, Costume Society, 1980

Foster, V., *The Visual History of Costume: The Nineteenth Century*, Batsford, 1984

de Gary M.N., ed., *Les Fouquet, Bijoutiers et Joailliers à Paris 1860-1960*, Paris, 1983

Gere, C., *Victorian Jewellery Design*, Kimber, 1972

Gernsheim, A., *Victorian and Edwardian Fashion: A Photographic Survey*, Dover, New York, 1981

Ginsburg, M., *Victorian Dress in Photographs*, Batsford, 1982

Grass, M.N., *A History of Hosiery*, Fairchild Publications Inc, 1955

Hinks, P., *Nineteenth Century Jewellery*, Faber, 1975

Hinks, P., *Twentieth Century British Jewellery*, Faber, 1983

Howell, G., *In Vogue: Six Decades of Fashion*, Allen Lane, 1975

Hull, W., *History of the Glove Trade*, London, 1834

Lewis, M., *Antique Paste Jewellery*, Faber, 1970

Mackrell, A., *Shawls, Stoles and Scarves*, Batsford, 1986

Marquardt, B., *Schmuck Klaasizismus und Biedermeier 1780-1850*, Munich, 1983

Mayor, S., *Collecting Fans*, Studio Vista, London, 1980

McDowell, C., *McDowell's Directory of Twentieth Century Fashion*, Frederick Muller, 1984

Muller, P., *Jewels in Spain 1500-1800*, New York, 1972

Munn G., *Castellani, Giuliano and Revivalist Jewellery in the Nineteenth Century*, London, 1984

Murdoch, T.(ed.), *Treasures and Trinkets*, Museum of London, 1991

Newman, Harold, *An Illustrated Dictionary of Jewellery*, Thames and Hudson, 1981

Ribeiro, A., *A Visual History of Costume: The Eighteenth Century*, Batsford, 1983

Ribeiro, A., *Dress in Eighteenth Century Europe 1715-1789*, Batsford, 1984

Ribeiro, A. and Cumming, V., *The Visual History of Costume*, Batsford, 1989

Rutt, R., *A History of Hand Knitting*, Batsford, 1987

Scarisbrick, D., *Jewellery*, Batsford, 1984

Staniland, K., *Fans*, Museum of London, 1985

Swann, J., *A History of Shoe Fashions*, Northampton Museum, 1975

Swann, J., *Shoes*, Batsford, 1982

Turner Wilcox, R., *The Mode in Hats and Headdress*, Scribners, New York, 1959

Walters Art Gallery, Baltimore, *Jewellery Ancient to Modern*, New York, 1979

Zucker, B., *Gems and Jewels, A Connoisseur's Guide*, Thames and Hudson, 1984

Museums to visit

Austria

MUSEUM FÜR VOLKERKUNDE, Vienna
OSTERREICHISCHES MUSEUM FÜR ANGEWANDTE KUNST
(FIGDOR COLLECTION), Vienna

Belgium

MUSÉES ROYAUX D'ART ET D'HISTOIRE, Brussels

Canada

BATA SHOE MUSEUM, Toronto
THE ROYAL ONTARIO MUSEUM, Toronto

France

MUSÉE DE L'ARLETAN, Arles
MUSÉE DES ARTS DECORATIFS, Bordeaux
MUSÉE DE LA SOIE, Lyon
MUSÉE DU TEXTILE, Lyon
MUSÉE LYONNAIS DES ARTS DECORATIFS, Lyon
MUSÉE HISTORIQUE DES TISSUS, Lyon
MUSÉE CARNAVALET, Paris
MUSÉE DE L''HOTEL DE CLUNY, Paris
MUSÉE DE LA MODE ET DU COSTUME, Paris
MUSÉE DU PRIEURE ST GERMAIN-EN-LAYE
MUSÉE OBERKAMPF, Jouy-en-Josas
MUSÉE DE L'IMPRESSION SUR ETOFFES, Mulhouse

Germany

MUSEUM FÜR VOLKERKUNDE, Berlin
MUSEUM FÜR KUNSTHANDWERK, Frankfurt
MUSEUM FÜR KUNST UND GEWERBE, Hamburg
ATONER MUSEUM, Hamburg
GERMANISCHES NATIONALMUSEUM, Nuremburg

Great Britain

WADDESDON MANOR, nr Aylesbury
MUSEUM OF COSTUME, Bath
CITY MUSEUM AND ART GALLERY, Birmingham
MUSEUM AND ART GALLERY, Brighton
MUSEUM & ART GALLERY, Bristol
FITZWILLIAM MUSEUM, Cambridge
MUSEUM OF WELSH LIFE, St Fagans, Cardiff
PICKFORD'S HOUSE MUSEUM, Derby
NATIONAL MUSEUM OF ANTIQUITIES, Edinburgh
ROYAL ALBERT MEMORIAL MUSEUM, Exeter
FARNHAM MUSEUM, Wilmer House, Farnham
GLASGOW MUSEUM & ART GALLERY, Glasgow
BURRELL COLLECTION, Glasgow
TEMPLE NEWSAM HOUSE, Leeds
LEICESTERSHIRE MUSEUMS, ART GALLERIES AND RECORDS
SERVICE, Leicester
VICTORIA & ALBERT MUSEUM, London
THE BRITISH MUSEUM, London
THE MUSEUM OF LONDON, London
HORNIMAN MUSEUM, London
MUSEUM OF MANKIND, London
LUTON MUSEUM, Luton
GALLERY OF ENGLISH COSTUME, Manchester
LAING ART GALLERY & MUSEUM, Newcastle
MUSEUMS & ART GALLERY, Northampton
STRANGERS HALL MUSEUM, Norwich
MUSEUM OF COSTUME AND TEXTILES, Nottingham
ASHMOLEAN MUSEUM, Oxford
PITT RIVERS MUSEUM, Oxford
PAISLEY MUSEUM AND ART GALLERIES, Paisley
HARRIS MUSEUM AND ART GALLERY, Preston
READING MUSEUM & ART GALLERY, Reading
THE WORTHING MUSEUM, Sussex
YORK CASTLE MUSEUM, York

Italy

Museo Stibbert, Florence
Castello Sforcesco, Milan
Museo Poldi Pozzoli, Milan
National Museum, Naples
Museo di Arte Orientale, Rome
Museo di Palazzo Venezia, Rome
Museo Correr, Venice

Netherlands

Rijksmuseum, Amsterdam
Museum Boyans van Benningen, Rotterdam

Portugal

Museu Nacional dos Coches, Lisbon

Spain

Museo de Indumentara (Colecion Rocamora), Barcelona
Museo Cambô, Barcelona
Palacio Fernan Nuñez, Madrid
Palacio Real di Aranjuez, nr Madrid

Sweden

National Museum, Stockholm

Switzerland

Kirschgarten Museum, Basel
Historisches Museum, Basel
Musée d'Art et d'Histoire, Geneva
Chateau de Nyon, Nyon
Schweizerisches Landemuseum, Zurich

United States of America

Museum of Fine Arts, Boston
Los Angeles County Museum of Art, Los Angeles
Brooklyn Museum, New York
Fashion Institute of Technology, New York
The Metropolitan Museum of Art, New York
Smithsonian Institution, Washington

Index and glossary

A select glossary of terms used in the text, with numbers which refer to an appropriate illustration

Aigrette a tuft of feathers, or of flowers or jewels, worn as a ornament in the hair
(f) 139

Balmoral boots an ankle boot with a closed front and a golosh (q.v.)
(f) 145

Bandeau a narrow band of fabric or jewellery worn round the head, usually across the forehead, but, when a hat across the hair
(f) 142, 170

Beaver yarn spun from the fur of this European rodent and its North American cousin; used in the production of hats, but also for stockings
(m) 46

Boa long round scarf or tippet, often made of feathers or fur
(f) 150

Boater a stiff straw hat with a shallow crown and straight brim
(f) 131

Bonnet general term for headwear, excluding hats, but, in the nineteenth century, the usual term for a close-fitting woman's 'hat'; a number of named variants became popular, such as the Bibi, Empire, Fanchon, Poke
(f) 87, 88, 96, 102, 110, 135

Boot a covering for foot and part of the leg
(f) 109, 138
(m) 8, 10, 62, 80

Boothose an overstocking or detachable band with an embroidered or decorated edge turned down over a boot
(m) 8, 13

Bowler hat a hard felt hat with domed crown and rolled brim
(m) 115, 164, 166

Bracelet item of jewellery closely or loosely fitted around the wrist
(f) 86, 91, 94, 102

Buckle a clasp comprising a rectangular or curved rim with one or more movable tongues secured to the chape at one side or in the middle, and long enough to rest on the opposite side. Used to fasten straps on shoes, breeches, etc., and ranging from simple metal to examples set with precious or semi-precious stones
(f/m) 38, 39, XVII

Buffon a large, often square neckerchief of fine material swathed around the neck and puffed out over the bosom
(f) 52, 54

Cameo a hard stone on which a design is cut to stand out in relief
(f) 73, 84, 145

Cap a closely fitting head-covering of unstructured material with an optional brim or edging
(f) 5, 18, 37, 43, I
(m) 43, 111, 163, 164, 166, I

Chapeau bras a crescent-shaped opera hat which could be folded flat
(m) 62, 63

Chatelaine an item of jewellery worn suspended from the waist, essentially a belt hook with chains to which keys, needlework, tools, watches and so forth were attached
(f) 122, 126

Chatelaine bag a style of bag which resembled in its attachment to the waist, and its construction, a chatelaine
(f) 122, 124, 125

Chevening fine embroidery on machine-knitted hose
(f/m) 68

Clock vertical decoration over the ankle on a stocking, embroidered or knitted
(1, 32)

Cocked hat a hat cocked into an equilateral triangle with the point worn at the front; named varieties included the Kevenhuller
(m) 18, 37, 43, 44, 46, 62

Coif a closely fitting cap sometimes tied under the chin
(f) 2

Pompon ornament for the hair or cap, of flowers and jewels
(f) 48

Pork pie hat a hat with a low, flat crown of straw and velvet, with a narrow brim turned up close all round
(f) 116

Pouch a bag or wallet suspended from the girdle or belt
(m) 4

Purse initially a pouch and then a small bag for carrying money
(f/m) 3, 15, 58, 72, 130, VII

Reticule/ridicule terms used to describe the bags used by women in the early nineteenth century
(f) 77, 84, 86, 89, 105

Round hat initially a soft man's hat which, for informal occasions, replaced the cocked hat in the 1770s; a female version appeared in the 1850s
(f) 103
(m) 82

Sandals a type of informal footwear which has straps or various cut-out sections over the foot
(f) 69, 180, XVII

Sash a rectangle of soft material, similar to a scarf (q.v.) the ends tied together
(m) 18

Scarf a narrow strip of material worn for warmth or decoration around the neck and falling over the shoulders
(f) 18, 56, 75, 145, 171, 172
(m) 163

Shawl a large square or rectangular scarf or wrap or cover to shoulders andupper body
(f) 60, 75, 81, 83, 91, 94, 98, 104, 110, 113, 115, 140, 145, 156, 160, IX, X

Shoe a covering for the foot, usually a leather sole with a fabric or leather upper; the shape, style, heel or lack of it vary considerably at different periods
(f) 6, 18, 34, 51, 69, 86, 91, 121, 127, 179, V, XVII
(m) 7, 18, 22, 38, 44, 82, 155, XVII

Shoe roses large decorative rosettes of ribbon or lace, sometimes decorated with spangles, which were fixed to the front of the shoe
(f/m) 1, 5

Socks a short stocking, principally worn by men after the introduction of pantaloons and trousers
(f) 173
(m) 175

Sovereign purse a container, of metal or other firm material, designed to hold this type of coin
(f/m) 130

Spangles small discs of shining metal, used to trim clothing and accessories; not dissimilar to modern sequins
(f/m) 5, 9, 19, 49, 59, 61, 64

Spats a short, buttoned, half-gaiter made of canvas cloth, worn with men's shoes
(m) 155, 163

Sticks the structure of thin supports holding or threaded through a fan leaf
(f) 36, 41, 47, 49, 78, 99, 129, 141

Stocking a close-fitting covering for the foot and leg
(f) 5, 68, 94, 108, 120, 134, 149, 178, XIII
(m) 65, 80, II
(f/m) 12, 32

Stomacher brooches
a graduated series of jewelled clasps worn on the front of a bodice
(f) 23, 48, IV

Stove-pipe hat a variant of the top hat
(m) 110

Straight(s) description of the style of shoe which was constructed to fit either foot
(f/m) 7, 19, 31, 38, 51, 69

Sweetbag a small embroidered bag, often scented, thus the word 'sweet'
(f/m) 3

Tiara raised hair ornament, usually of graduated size; simple or heavily decorated and set with gemstones, pearls, etc.
(f) 73, 75

Tie pockets a pair of pockets held together by a tape and worn under the skirt
(f) 53

Tippet a short shoulder cape
(f) 18, 66

Top hat a tall, high-crowned hat, usually with a shallow up-curved brim; the principal formal hat for men throughout the nineteenth century and into the twentieth century
(m) 70, 79, 82, 111, 112, 145, 164

Toque a close-fitting turban style hat without a brim
(f) 150

Trilby hat a soft black hat with a wide brim, named after the late nineteenth-century play of the same name in which this was worn by a principal character
(m) 145, 164

Tufts small decorative tassels found on clothing and accessories such as gloves
(f/m) 23, 26)

Umbrella at first a sunshade for women, then later, when water-proofed, used mainly to protect against rain while parasols (q.v.) were used in sunshine
(f) 137, 177
(m) 28, 56, 57, 79, 80, 82, 84, 110, 114, 122, 137

Utility mark CC41 was stamped or woven into all goods which required coupons for purchase; it was introduced in 1941 and finally abolished in 1952
(f/m) 173, 174, 178

Vellum calfskin specially treated to form a thin, paper-like material and used for early fan leaves
(f) 45, 49

Wallet purse a long tubular purse which emerged at the end of the eighteenth century, also known later as a miser, ring and stocking purse
(f/m) 55, 102, 119, VII

Watch a portable time-piece, often a highly decorative item of jewellery which was usually round and suspended from a chain; later applied to wrist watches also
(m) 70

Wellington boot named after the Duke, a top boot without a turnover top
(m) 79, 82

Wide-awake hat a broad-brimmed, low-crowned felt hat usually worn in the country
(m) 110